To Cassidy and Daniel - you are the wealth, joy, and meaning in my life.

First Published in 2012 by *Innovation Publishing*

A division of Ms Independence Pty Ltd, Australia

National Library of Cataloguing-in-Publication data:

Author: Cydney Turner

Title: *Fast Money Magic! 108 Legal Ways to Get Quick Cash*/ Cydney Turner

ISBN: 978-1-922093-02-8

Subjects: Home Business, Money and Finance

Editing by: WickedCopy

Photo credit: ©Depositphotos/ Yuri Arcurs

For general information on our other products and services, please find our contact information online at www.MillionairesAcademy.com

To purchase customized or bulk copies of this book, please visit us online at www.MillionairesAcademy.com/bulk

Table of Contents

Acknowledgments

The original ideas in this book actually came from my own life experiences, and those of about 30 of my dear and most inspiring friends.

But there are four really important people that I want to thank from the bottom of my heart. The first is my editor Kathryn Calhoun, who is wonderful. She has supported and believed in my dream to help women worldwide, and stuck with it and me for years and years! Her belief in me and her support of this project has sometimes been the life buoy that has kept it alive when life has kicked me in the guts.

Kathryn has poured months into this book and brought it to life too. She is simply brilliant and if you need an excellent writer or editor, I can recommend her most highly after working with her on so many projects. You can find her at her own successful online business, www.WickedCopy.ca.

I'd also like to thank my team, Nancy for her weeks of dedication and creativity, and the wonderful Jay and Liliana, who did a fabulous job with the layout and cover over and over until we had all the little things right enough to go to print. This book was written to help people find fast solutions, so we wanted to get it to print as quickly as possible.

The third person I'd like to thank is my dear mother, Gail, because she taught me everything that I really needed to know to live a life of success, joy, and celebration. She then taught my children to love books and the joy of reading, which has brought them so much success and pleasure in their lives.

She also helped me write the first draft of this work and the night she broke down all my long, long sentences into ones that allowed a breath, we laughed so much the tears were flowing. It was one of the best nights of my life, and I thank her for helping me meet that deadline and so many others with her incredible organizational skills and devotedly standing over me until I got my groove on!

Michael O'Sullivan also deserves a special thank you. I haven't always been the easiest person to co-parent with – I'm pretty out there with my big dreams and gypsy lifestyle. But when I went through my tough times and really needed support and friendship, he was one of the very few who really made me welcome, let me wallow in my grief but not for too long, sat in those bank and lawyers' meetings with me, and showed me what a gentleman and truly loyal and caring friend is.

I'd also like to acknowledge all the wonderful people who contributed to this book, too many to mention, though you will meet some through their generous contributions and stories dedicated with love to you. It's true that if you want a job done, you ask a busy person – the contributors to this book are some of the busiest people I know, but they still found time to help out.

When YOU make it to the end of this book, then I acknowledge you too – for being a champion and caring enough to take a chance – you really deserve fast money and all the rewards it brings. Remember to let us know how it works out for you! The biggest shame would be if you let this opportunity go to waste, and did nothing at all. Pick one thing and become a master at that and this can be the day you change your life for GOOD!

My mother has taught me so much about how much the quality of our lives is affected by the choices we make every day, and whether we choose to be a champion of life or a victim focused on blame and complaining. Of course, she had a fair bit of complaining to do about my dad, but to her credit, she didn't let it stop her having an incredible adventure and a truly amazing life. She met and married another brilliant man, and together they built a business that gave us a wonderful lifestyle while both worked full-time jobs.

My mother gave us an extraordinary foundation in life, an incredible education and self-reliance skills that have seen us through many hardships. I'm sure you'll agree that at some stage of our lives we all have challenges and adversities, and some people seem to get more than their fair share. They have one bad experience after another, and some come out of it like heroes while others can end up beaten down and broken. But it is our ability to continuously improve our lives through the decision to be resilient and resourceful that has inspired this book, and I really hope you will get as much inspiration from it as I did putting these ideas together.

If I did it, I know you can too....

Because of the excellent work ethic I learned from my parents, I have gone from strength to strength in my career and have been so blessed. I have had so much success in life that I felt compelled to share my blessings. I have the most incredible network of friends, many of whom are successful business builders and caring, generous mentors and educators. So I asked them all to give me their best ideas for ways to make money fast. This book is packed full of their ideas and tips based on their life experiences as well as my own.

I have worked for mostly small to medium enterprises that were very, very profitable and successful since before I left high school, scoring my first summer job with a television ad producer who went on to ultimately own TV stations of his own in China. I am an experienced business renovator and bought my first turnaround 'shop' based business in 1987. I started with a small sandwich delivery business and have since owned cafés, caterers, boutiques, gift shops, been a clothing designer and retailer, stock market and real estate investor, property developer and now Internet marketer and book publisher! My businesses have made me millions and business really can do the same for you.

Writing books has been a dream of mine since childhood, and now, writing books to help others find success in their lives is my adult dream come true! As I put the final touches to this book before it goes to print, I am already designing the education program for my next book, based on interviews with millionaires to discover their 'fast millionaire formulas.' I congratulate you for buying and reading this book and I hope you will get inspired by at least one of over 100 ideas to create a new income stream in your life. Definitely sign up for our newsletter so we can share the fast millionaire tips with you as soon as we can!

Where should you start?

There are over 100 great ideas in this book, many of which should get you thinking about a small business you can start in your spare time, something that is a fit for you and that you can really get passionate about. If you just get started, the next book in our series will really help you along. It will be detailed, step-by-step instructions on how to take that business to the next level and lay the foundations for a wonderful income generating and life changing future... as big as you dare to dream!

Make sure you get your money's worth with this book - please come to our website, www.MillionairesAcademy.com, and join our newsletter (you'll get some other great books as our gift to you when you do). You'll get ongoing free tips and tricks to bring money into your life easily and flowingly. I know there's a massive amount of information coming at you already, so please let me filter some of it for you into tested, proven, easy to use strategies that you can implement just a little bit each week and really turn your life around in no time at all!

Why should you believe me?

I started my first job and my first business with no cash at all and with hard work and frugal living built up a nice little fortune.

When I started this book I was rolling in dough – I had lots of homes and investment properties, millions of dollars in shares of some of the best companies in my country and was living the life of luxury.

But with the millions I was earning, I thought I could hand over the responsibility for the management of my most important assets to fancy advisors. Then I compounded the earnings by investing in some private businesses and funds that I really didn't understand or have control over. Then just before the financial crisis of 2008, which has so drastically impacted the economies on a massive scale around the entire world, I realized that my own hard-earned fortune was in severe danger.

I was lucky to catch it in time to sell off almost everything before the collapse that would have left me wiped out financially. When the dust settled, I had lost the bulk of the wealth I'd spent 20 years building. The shock of losing everything in just a couple of years hit me in the form of devastating depression and anxiety. However, my wonderful children and family kept reminding me that although I may have lost some zeros, I still had the true wealth in my life: the people I love, my health, and all my life experience.

I had really hit what felt like rock bottom. But then I turned it around and rebuilt my business to something that brings me far greater joy than what I was doing before. I now feel far less burdened, and confident that what people say is true: success can be duplicated. When you have done it once, you can do it over and over again, as long as you know and believe that you can.

You deserve to have a wonderful life, and so do all the people you love. In fact, if I can inspire you to help some others too, then I will really have accomplished my goal. My mission in life is to spread hope and joy and improve the lives of as many people as possible while I am still young enough to make a difference!

Remember where I came from? I was a little girl whose mother couldn't give her time or toys, only love and a commitment to a bright future. Well, I know how far those two ingredients can be stretched – and I hope you will join me in sharing the love.

Please come to our website and let me know how you have used these ideas and strategies in your own life. Sharing your journey and experiences inspires us and helps others.

To your brilliant life,

~Cydney Turner
Dream it! Live it! Love it! ®

PS. If you have just one positive, motivated friend who genuinely wants to make fast money too, then forming a money club (check out Tip #37) can really catapult you along. But please, don't let them hold you back from getting started on your own bright future - the fastest way to your bright new future is FORWARD!! In order for something to change *for* you – something must change *with* you!

Chapter 1: A New Beginning!

Take a breath and relax. Your money problems are coming to an end.

Okay, I know it's not easy, especially when all you can think about is how much money you wish you had, how much you need. I know what you're going through. I have been there.

This book is full of fabulous ideas and inspiration to make more money, save more money, and find more money in ways you may have not yet considered. I have a lot to say in this book - and I've rallied many of my financial expert friends to lend their advice, too. Some of the advice that follows will be said several times in different ways because everyone learns and absorbs things differently.

If you need money fast, I'm sure you're wondering, "Can I really do this? And how?" Well, rest assured that the next 200-plus pages are going to offer you a lot of ideas and inspiration. YES, you can do this! But before we get down to the "how," I'd like you to first look at the "whys" and "whens" of your particular situation.

Why did you pick up this book?

Your "why" is always one of the strongest motivators behind any action you take, so it's wise to get a handle on the specific reasons you're seeking to find more money in your life. Make your reasons clear and don't be afraid to dream big! They are what will inspire you in your goal towards finding more money... fast.

Why do you want the money? What problems of yours will it solve? What benefits will it bring to you? How will it benefit others? How will it make you feel? Making a list is a great idea here. The more powerful your reasons, the easier and more enjoyable it will be to reach your goals. Write out your "whys" and post them somewhere where you can look at them often for extra motivation and inspiration.

When will you succeed?

Yikes - this question probably sounds a little daunting, especially if you're overwhelmed by money woes.

A step-by-step approach is the key. Clear deadlines or milestones are helpful for most people; that way you can celebrate each small goal along the way to help keep your determination high. Also remember to set that larger, more exciting goal for yourself, so you'll remember that the bigger picture of financial freedom is waiting for you!

The biggest part of your "when" will depend on you, but the power of external support and accountability cannot be underestimated. If you can, get a partner to share the Fast Money Magic journey with you, to help you face your challenges, keep on track, and stay inspired.

Ready? Let's get to it!

Tip #1: Learn the Art of Wealthy Thinking

If you're struggling with money issues, you may think that the concept of wealth as a mindset is totally unrealistic. However, once you do succeed in developing an overall attitude of wealth, you'll be astonished by how your old habit of negative thinking was sabotaging your ability to create abundant cash flow in your life.

The fact of the matter is that your thought patterns about money *do* affect the way you generate income. If you tell yourself on a daily basis that you allow money to come to you and that you invite money into your life, I promise you'll start to see some real changes in short order.

To assist you in your development of a wealthy mindset, read the classics *Think and Grow Rich* by Napoleon Hill, *The Science of Getting Rich* by Wallace Wattles, and *The Secret* by Rhonda Byrne (also available on DVD). These books describe how you can use positive thinking to attract wealth and good fortune into your life. Each of these books was a true inspiration to me on my journey toward riches and I am sure they will have a positive impact on your path, as well.

Some of these books and videos may not be your cup of tea; however, if you are committed to a healthy financial life, there is no debating that it all starts with the development of wealthy thinking. You'll find that each and every one of the books above are unbelievably inspirational - and you should never, ever underestimate the power of being inspired.

It is worth exploring some of these avenues (that ultimately all lead to the same basic and simple premise) to start cultivating a mindset of abundant wealth. You will see that money is really nothing more than energy that sustains us through this physical journey and, by aligning yourself with that energy (or vibration), you will be able to attract not only money, but anything else you desire.

The vibration that you emitted yesterday, last month, last year, and for your whole life up until now has led to the physical reality that you are experiencing today. Like attracts like. What you have now or what you feel you are missing in life is the direct result of the vibrations you activated by your beliefs.

The best news is that if you aren't thrilled with where you are in your life, financially or otherwise, your reality can be changed by shifting your beliefs. As I mentioned before, if your "whys" are strong enough, important enough, powerful enough, you won't be able to overlook the fact that wealthy thinking is a crucial element of manifesting wealth. Not only will the ideas flow and the opportunities show up, but the actual money will start to arrive - perhaps even sooner than you think is possible right now. As an added bonus, you will begin to feel a lot lighter and happier as you learn to take charge of your thoughts, beliefs and, by natural extension, your life.

My next book, *Social Wealth Secrets*, is also full of ideas for creating wealth. It includes advice from successful social entrepreneurs, skill-building tips and techniques, and the practical advice you need to master business and create

between the two sides of our brains and shift our energies in a very positive way. When your brain is stimulated in this manner, you are able to learn and access information more readily than if you were simply reading it. Famous movie director Stephen Spielberg has revealed that some of his best film ideas have come to him while driving!

Whatever you choose to do, remember that getting out of your money crisis and increasing your cash flow is a rewarding but ongoing process that requires your constant vigilance. The activities and readings suggested here are great ways to maintain your involvement and awareness about your financial situation and your plans to improve it. As long as you continue to educate yourself about wealthy thinking, your money situation will continue to improve. Keep at it! Debt-free, cash-positive living is just around the corner!

Tip #3: Taking Stock - Your Personal Net Worth

Any successful project begins with planning. Although it isn't usually as fun or exciting as dreaming or goal setting, it's the cornerstone upon which you will build your financial success.

Your planning begins with taking stock of where you are and what it is that you already have, which includes both your income streams as well as your money drains. Use the pages that follow as a worksheet (don't be afraid to write in this book!) to help you get a clearer idea of your current net worth:

My Net Worth Tracking Sheet

MY ASSETS

Cash & Liquid Assets

Cash and bank accounts .... $____

Bonds, term deposits, investments .... $____

Money owed to me .... $____

Other .... $____

Marketable Assets

Mutual funds .... $____

Stocks .... $____

Real estate investments .... $____

Business interests .... $____

Other .... $____

Long-Term Assets

RRSP, 401K, superannuation fund, etc. .... $____

Cash value of life insurance .... $____

Pension plans, profit sharing .... $____

Other .... $____

Personal Assets

Residence .... $____

Recreational property .... $____

Other real estate .... $____

Vehicles .... $____

Recreational equipment .... $____

Household furnishings and equipment .... $____

Collectibles .... $____

Other .... $____

MY TOTAL ASSETS = $______________

MY LIABILITIES

Short-Term Debt

Charge accounts, credit cards .... $____

Lines of Credit .... $____

Loans .... $____

Unpaid Bills .... $____

Taxes .... $____

Other .... $____

Long-Term Debt

Mortgage .... $____

Other .... $____

MY TOTAL LIABILITIES = $__________

NET WORTH:

TOTAL ASSETS - TOTAL LIABILITIES = $______

Thoughts About My Net Worth:

Sometimes – for some, often - this exercise is confronting. But remember your commitment to wealthy thinking and refuse to get down about the not-so-great aspects of your net worth! Instead, challenge yourself to use this book as a tool to transform your personal financial picture. Let the numbers you see motivate you to create your happier, healthier, wealthier life!

If you're still feeling stressed or upset about what you have just charted, consider this: you are now in the elite minority of those who choose to take charge of their finances (and their lives). You have already taken the first difficult steps

MY TOTAL INCOME = $____________

MY EXPENSES

Housing

Mortgage/Rent .... $____

Property taxes .... $____

Home maintenance .... $____

Heat, power, water .... $____

Telephone, internet, cable .... $____

Furniture, housekeeping, etc. .... $____

Other housing expenses .... $____

Credit

Student loan payments .... $____

Car loan payments .... $____

Line of credit payments .... $____

Credit card fees .... $____

Other credit payments .... $____

Living Expenses

Groceries .... $____

Eating out .... $____

Coffee breaks/Snacks .... $____

Alcohol .... $____

Pet expenses .... $____

Clothing .... $____

Personal grooming .... $____

Entertainment .... $____

Other .... $____

Transportation

Fuel .... $____

Public transit .... $____

Taxis .... $____

Parking .... $____

Driver's license fees.. $____

Repairs/maintenance .... $____

Other .... $____

Insurance

Home insurance .... $____

Auto insurance .... $____

Health insurance.. $____

Dental costs .... $____

Copays .... $____

Eyeglasses/Contacts/Eye care .... $____

Prescriptions .... $____

Life insurance .... $____

Other .... $____

Miscellaneous

Gym memberships .... $____

Fitness classes .... $____

Subscriptions .... $____

Vacations .... $____

Charities .... $____

Gifts .... $____

Other .... $____

MY TOTAL Expenses = $ ______________

Thoughts About My Income and Expenses:

If you're having trouble filling out the info above, you aren't alone. It can be hard to keep track of how much you're spending in all of those categories! However, spending is a part of life and it's important to be able to understand where your money is coming from and where it's going.

To get a better handle on what's up with your income and expenses, start tracking your daily expenses. Take a small notepad with you whenever you go shopping and make a note of what you spend, or keep your receipts and do it when you get home. If you can manage to track your expenditures for a whole month, then you'll be able to slot everything into the worksheet above and get a good idea of where your money is going.

Ideally, your income should be greater than your expenses so that you can put money towards your retirement, credit card debt, or rainy day fund. If it isn't, don't panic. Your financial picture is already in the process of changing for the better!

Tip #5: Building Your Budget

If you aren't thrilled with how your income and expenses turned out on the worksheet above, now is the time to start making changes.

Start by taking another look at your worksheet and seeing where you could tweak your spending habits. Some things like health insurance or public transit fees might not be

to make something else - in this case, money. When you're worried about money, it's easy to forget what resources you have, so you may have to spend some time to get those creative juices flowing. Once the ideas begin to flow, don't be surprised if they start coming more and more quickly, one after the other. Prepare to be inspired!

On a fresh sheet of paper, list all of your resources, skills, contacts, and networks. If you aren't sure where to begin, take a look at some of the ideas below for inspiration:

Your Potential Resources

Do you have gently used furniture that you don't need anymore? Perhaps it can be sold. Do you have extra space in your house that you don't need? Perhaps it could be rented out for accommodation, office space, or storage. Do you have any days that you regularly leave your car sitting in the driveway? Maybe a neighbor could use it that day for errands. Use your imagination as you look around and assess the resources in your life.

Your Skills

Are you good at painting fences? Do you have a knack for bartering? Could you offer child care? What can you do well that may be of value to someone else? You might be surprised just how much monetary value is hiding within your skills and/or hobbies. A little self-promotion might be all it takes to get that extra cash rolling in.

Your Contacts and Networks

Do you know someone who would recommend you for a job? Do you belong to clubs, groups, or associations that you can mine for help? If so, begin by checking out any bulletin boards they might have that advertise a need for a good or service. Also, don't forget about the person you enlisted to keep you motivated on your path to wealth; he or she is an invaluable contact who will provide you not just with support, but likely wealth-building ideas and inspiration, too.

Dig deep in order to come up with every last resource at your disposal. You might find it better to have a friend or two to work with on this with you because they may be able to identify ideas that you don't right away. It's only natural: people tend not to think at their clearest when they have money worries.

Tip #7: The Sneaky Resources You're Forgetting

One resource you may be overlooking is any cash you currently have in the bank. Is that money working for you? You don't need to dive into super high-risk investments to grow that money - you simply need to choose a bank that offers higher interest rates than the competition. Check out Internet banking companies - they're as safe as their land-based competitors, but because of their low overhead, they are able to offer their customers attractive interest rates, even on checking accounts. All it takes on your end is a little online research and then the simple act of moving your money from one account to another; you'll be making additional, regular interest income with no ongoing effort on your part. Talk about working smarter and not harder! Just be sure that whomever you choose to look after your money is reliable and insured.

Another resource that may have escaped your notice is your job. If you have a job, there is a good chance you could be doing something there to earn more money. Could you be putting in more hours? Many jobs pay time-and-a-half for overtime hours, so even one extra shift a week could make a big difference in your paycheck. Or perhaps it's time to ask for a raise. If your bosses are impressed with your work, a simple conversation highlighting your contributions - with a note about how you're having a bit of trouble making ends meet - may be all it takes to make more for every hour you put in. Finally, remember that the experience you have from your job is a resource too, so if you aren't making as much as you should, it might be time to move on to a job that pays you what you're worth.

When identifying your resources, it's worth spending about 60 percent of your available time and energy working out what resources you have and which will likely give you the best return for your efforts. The other 40 percent should be you taking action to make the best of the resources you've uncovered. In a money crunch, you don't want to waste time going down a dead-end path that could have been avoided with a little more planning. Remember the proverb: "Measure twice, cut once."

Tip #8: Expert Insight From Cheyne Goulden

Internet Marketer and Real Estate Investor Cheyne Goulden, from Melbourne, Australia, Weighs in on Creating Wealth Fast:

If I had to make money fast, how would I do it? This is the same formula that I used with one client in the property investment space to make over $ 300,000 in one weekend.

The 5W/5H Formula:

1. *Why? I get a clear picture of my "why." In order to create a large amount of money in the shortest time possible, the first step would be to get a really good grasp on "why." Why do I want it? What good is it going to cause in the world when I achieve this? What will the ripple effect be for other people all over the world? I write down all the things that it would mean to me. I write down the pleasure I would get from hitting the goal and the pain from not getting it in as much detail as I can.*
2. *What? I get specific on my outcome. How much money do I want to make? I come up with my key metrics and a visual image of the goal and stick it all around my home and office.*
3. *Who? I make a commitment with three of my peers whom I respect most via www.stickK.com. This allows*

me to share my goal with people that I care about and opens me up to endless derision should I not follow through. It also provides me with accountability and additional support. I also get at least one person to donate a few days of their time to help me and offer to give them 10 percent of whatever was created. This person would serve as a team member to help fill any skill gaps or just provide some moral support and accountability. Magic happens when two or more minds meet in collaboration.

5. *When? I give myself a clear deadline for the achievement of this goal. I also include a lock-down mode for at least two to three days of intense focus, planning and execution. I find a way to get out of my normal environment. This helps to break some old patterns.*
6. *How? (Part 1) Get massive leverage to kick your old vibration and raise your energy. This step gives me the fuel I need to get the "how" cracking.*
7. *I remember a story that one of my mentors, Stuart Wilde, told that stuck with me so vividly from many years ago. He said that people buy your energy so if you want more money, you need to raise your life force energy. Then people will show up so you gotta get organized so that you can bill 'em! He went on to say that from an esoteric point of view it is important to jolt your current vibration and put sufficient energy to kick up to a new level of energy and vibration. He*

continued to say, "Imagine that you are swimming in a lake and all of a sudden a 'Swamp Thing' grabs you by the ankle and drags you down to the murky depths of the deep abyss. "How hard would you kick to get free from the grips of the 'Swamp Thing?' That's how hard you need to kick to break out of the vibration that you are currently holding." How much of your energy and focus would be on kicking free? Would five to twenty percent cut it? Could you be checking Facebook watching a video at the same time as kicking free? Of course not. You would put 100 percent of your focus and energy into breaking free. That vibration you held yesterday created how much money you have today. It is important to become aware of your vibration. Is it heavy and low when it comes to money and your life in general? Right now pay attention to it. If it is heavy, feel the heaviness of the old vibration. Become really aware and conscious of it. Imagine how it would feel if this were to continue for another year, another 10 years. What do you look like when you see yourself in the mirror? What has it cost you? What have you missed out on? What has it cost your family and the ones you love most? The pain that you are feeling here is why you need to make a decision right now to kick free from this vibration. Right now is your moment of power to create a different vibration. So what you are really doing in the "kick" is raising your vibration and raising your energy. When you throw off the burden of the heavy stinky "Swamp Thing," you naturally rise back up to the surface of the abundant ocean where you can breathe in the fresh air and enjoy life. During this time (and for as long as I want to attract money) I develop a practice that increases my physical energy both from a diet and exercise perspective. I commit to devouring all sorts of super foods, green smoothies, I get out barefoot and run along the beach for an hour a day so I can connect to nature. I don't put anything into my body that lowers my vibration or dilutes my power during this "kick."

8. *How? (Part 2) I find a BIG problem in a market that I know something about and am passionate about. For instance, if I loved dogs and had a business in selling dog grooming information products, I would do some market research. I would speak to my customers in that market. I would read comments on popular YouTube videos that related to dogs. I would check out forums and see what people were talking about and what their problems were. I might survey my clients and ask them what their biggest challenges were when it came to looking after their dogs. I would also review the other products on the market to see where the gaps were.*

9. *How? (Part 3) I create compelling, unique content that solves the problem in an interesting fun way. I focus all my creative talent, skill, and energy on putting together a solution to the big problems. My focus is on totally giving massive value in a unique way to lots*

of people for FREE. I put each idea I have on a sticky note and then put them all on the wall. Then, I put two vertical lines down the middle of a whiteboard and say the ones on the left are GOOD KARMA, FREE YOUTUBE CONTENT. The ones in the middle are GOOD KARMA, FREE SUBSCRIBER CONTENT, and the ones on the right are BEST DAMN MASTER PAID CONTENT AROUND. Then I put roughly 10 percent of the material in the left category, 30 percent in the middle and 60 percent in the right. Continuing with the dog information products example, I would set about putting together my FREE YouTube video and FREE subscriber content into three videos that tackle the biggest issues and challenges that dog owners face. Each video would be from three to ten minutes in length and could be really simple, just using a slideshow and audio voiceover. I would focus on giving massive value and building incredible goodwill in the marketplace. I would use tools like the Video Boss or List Machine Pro to incorporate Facebook commenting underneath the videos. I would then put the other content into one low price point and one higher price point product. Now, if you are struggling for free content, remember that you don't have to create it all yourself.You can be the curator of content, in that you collect it from other places and put it together in a summary. If it's not easy to do, then you are doing it wrong.

10. *How? (Part 4) I send lots of people to my website. I set about sending as much traffic to the free video content pages as humanly possible. To get the dog content out there, I would ask people to make comments on their Facebook walls and find a way to get the videos going viral by joining Facebook groups, making friends, and contributing ideas. I would ask permission from moderators to post my videos on their pages. I'd also send emails to my database and ask people to start a joint venture with me and send to their mailing lists, as well. I would buy some traffic from Facebook once I had done some testing on the opt-in rate and had it above 10 percent.*
11. *How? (Part 5) I build a list of people who call me their trusted advisor. I ensure that I'm capturing their email addresses so that I am building a list to market to more easily than people with whom I have no relationship. I put these people on an autoresponder and get a pre-created sequence of emails over the first seven days to build even more rapport.*
12. *Bill 'Em! Turn those relationships into money. Going back to the dog example, once I had built massive goodwill with my market and delivered great content for free I would launch my advanced dog care and training program at 47 dollars (via video of course). This program might be a series of three longer videos going into more detail and include detailed PDF documents and cheat sheets as bonuses.They might*

also include audio files that someone can listen to when walking their dog. I would also have an upsell into a 297-dollar program. This would only be shown to people who purchased at the 47-dollar price point as a special offer. It might include some form of live training event or personal service such as a series of Skype sessions. I would have a down-sell of 9 dollars for a special trial version of the program with the balance paid in 14 days. If they didn't love the content and have best looking dog in town then they wouldn't pay a cent and they would get a free dog scratcher for their troubles. I would also have a seven-to-ten week coaching program. It may even have some live training. I would make it massive value. Make it practical. The idea is to make it worth 3,000 dollars and charge only 297 dollars, just one tenth of the price. You want to make your content compelling and risk-free so people eat it up.

Good luck!

Cheyne Goulden

www.netrepreneur.com.au

Tip #9: Add Positive Actions to Your Life Every Day

Since you now have the ball rolling, please do everything you can to maintain the momentum! Remember the law of inertia: an object in motion tends to remain in motion.

A delightfully simple way to keep building upon the progress you've already made is to take five actions every single day that will take you out of debt and toward the wealth that you desire. These can be very small acts, but they are nevertheless important because they will help you make wealth a lifelong habit.

I find that keeping a wealth journal is an inspirational way to track progress and stay focused. Use your journal to write down each of the five wealthy actions you've taken in a day as well as any other money saving ideas you come up with to use on other days. Start your journal today; when you look back over it in a month's time, you'll be amazed at how far you've come! Soon, your journal will also be full of ideas that you can use again and again to create your wealthy lifestyle.

If five actions seems like a lot, use this book for inspiration and remember that grand gestures are not necessary. For example, today you might make lunches for you and your family, cancel your expensive cable package, avoid the designer coffee shop, start cleaning out a closet for a garage sale, and take the kids on a free trip to the library. (Oh, and while you're at the library, be sure to pick up some of my recommended reading: that's one wealthy action that will last for at least several days!)

If you don't get to five positive actions every single day, don't fret and don't allow yourself to be discouraged. One positive action in a week is better than none at all. Just remember that every action you take for the benefit of your financial situation will only bring you closer to your debt-free, wealthy life. So get started right now!

Congratulations! You've just made it through a significant obstacle to wealth: getting started. Please don't underestimate the power of what you've accomplished. The journey to abundant riches is composed of small steps. Each one you take moves you nearer your goals and fondest dreams.

I hope you enjoy yourself along the way!

Chapter 2: What Will You Give Up for Cash?

A wealthy life starts with a wealthy lifestyle, but if you have a bunch of stuff cluttering up your life, it can be impossible to imagine there actually being room in your life for abundant wealth.

It's time to take a new approach to what you truly need in life. If you put your life under a "money microscope," you would likely see a whole bunch of little holes where money is simply falling out of your life.

If you're in a debt crisis, you need cash. I'm here to help you find it. You might be surprised to find that cash is just a few clever decisions away from you. Find your inspiration, hold on to your motivation, and get creative. It's time to start hunting for the cash that has been eluding you.

Tip #10: Sell Anything You Need Less Than Cash

Almost all of us have belongings we've been storing in our homes that we can exchange for cash or barter with to get something we need more. Many of us have a strong tendency to hang onto stuff we no longer use, "just in case." Of course, we all know that those "just in case" situations almost never arise, so it's time that you took a serious look at what you've got around the house that you could use to get you out of the tough spot you're in right now.

Go through your closets with a critical eye. Do you have clothes that you no longer wear or that you're hoping you'll fit into eventually? Do you have books you've already read (or will never read)? What about toys and clothing that your kids have outgrown? What about extra furniture that you don't use anymore? Don't neglect the storage areas of your house: your basement, attic, crawl spaces, etc. You might even have some big-ticket items like extra cars, appliances, or a property that you just can't afford right now.

If you're paying for a storage locker, commit to emptying it out. Not only can you potentially get cash for its contents, but the cost of renting the space will be one more expense you can say goodbye to for good.

I am a terrible pack rat, so believe me when I say that I know it can be hard to part with personal belongings. However, it is truly amazing how refreshing it is to clean out your closets and shelves and just generally rid your home of needless clutter. Plus, it not only takes away the stress of living in a jam-packed house, but imagine how you would feel if getting rid of that clutter could pay off a credit card or help you make a mortgage payment. Debt is such a tremendous worry; wouldn't it be better to use the items you don't need to lift that burden off your shoulders for good?

Once you've collected all the things you plan to sell, it's time to advertise. Many communities have newspapers in which you can place classified ads for free. If you've got a lot of things, you may want to have a garage sale (see our next tip for advice on hosting the most profitable garage sale ever.) You could also put up flyers in community halls or around your neighborhood to generate awareness about your items.

There are also online community classified ad sites such as Craigslist, Gumtree, Trading Post, Kijiji, eBay Classified Ads, etc. where you can list your items for sale for free. You'll probably be shocked at how easy it is to sell even the obscurest of items. These sites are generally extremely user friendly, so it's easy to create a free advertisement and even include a few photos of the items you have for sale. A concise and clear description of your item will go a long way in selling it, as will clear and simple photographs.

There is also a pretty interesting theory that telling the story behind an item will make it more attractive to potential buyers. Was that designer coat once worn to a celebrity gala? Was that pair of shoes worn the day you got hired for your dream job? Was that shawl worn by your grandmother on her wedding day?

A sentiment can go a long way in grabbing attention and making an item more interesting and more appealing. In some situations, it may also be beneficial to include a note in your advertisement explaining what you plan to use the money for. For example, if you happen to be selling your belongings to put your child through college or to pay off a medical debt, let people know. It will inspire them not only to purchase your items at full price, but perhaps to make a donation to your cause, as well.

There are so many wonderful benefits to getting rid of clutter. Of course you'll have a tidier home with more storage space. You'll certainly enjoy waving goodbye to some of your money troubles, as well. However, you'll also undoubtedly discover another benefit that you may not have thought of: less clutter and less debt usually means more space for creative thinking, fresh ideas, and a renewed optimism about your life. It might just be the new start you need to put even more of your financial woes far behind you.

Tip #11: Have a Garage Sale or Yard Sale

If you're wondering how you can bear to part with your belongings, go back to the previous section and have another read. Remember that your clutter-bug tendencies can only hurt your ability to reduce your financial worries. It's finally time to say goodbye to all that money stress!

Get together absolutely everything that you can stand to get rid of and have a great big garage sale. Turn those useless items into money in the bank; you'll be glad you did,

I promise. Whatever you don't sell you can take to a few flea markets or put groups of things together into bundles and offer them at irresistible prices. Make a goal for yourself that everything you choose to sell does not get to come back into your home.

Hold your garage sale on a weekend to maximize the amount of traffic you get. The morning of your sale, put up signs all over the community to advertise. All you need is poster paper in a bright color with your address, the dates and hours, and the words "garage sale" on each one. Make sure the writing is big enough and short enough for people to read in just a second or two. Put up lots of signs to generate as much awareness as possible about your sale and use arrows so drivers can follow your signs easily.

There are people out there who scout around for garage sale signs every single weekend, so make sure your sale gets noticed with these important tips:

- Use the same color of paper for each sign so people can easily identify and follow your signs.

- Put up posters in community centers, etc. a couple of days ahead of time to generate lots of awareness. Don't put up your directional signs till the day of to avoid them going "missing."

- Advertise for free online on community classified ad sites. Make sure you post in the "garage sale" category and consider posting on multiple days, if permitted by the site, so your ad doesn't get buried underneath newer ads.

- Consider advertising in your local newspaper and/or community magazine. Although they usually charge fees, sometimes they'll throw in price stickers, garage sale signs, and balloons to help promote your sale.

- Find out what the yard sale culture is in your area. Where I live, a cluster of colorful balloons hanging beside a sale sign is a clear indication that a yard sale is near. See what works in your neighborhood.

- Don't forget to put the hours on your sign to help avoid early birds. In any classified ads you place, include the words "no early birds" unless you want people knocking on your door at 7:00am.

- Make sure the wording on your directional signs is as large as possible and includes an arrow. The best signs look something like:

YARD SALE

MAPLE AT 12th

TODAY 9-3

→ → →

Tip #12: Running a Hugely Successful Garage Sale

The day before your sale, be sure to have all your items well organized. Use tables to display your items (you can create makeshift tables out of milk crates or sawhorses and a sheet of plywood). Try to group similar items together, so your customers will have an easier time shopping - and spending! Also, I find that pricing items is better than not. Some people simply aren't comfortable asking, "How much does this cost?" By making prices clear, you are inviting people to make offers. Price everything ahead of time so you aren't scrambling come garage sale day.

When the big day arrives, enjoy it! Every little bit of money you earn is a little more money than you had before. To ensure things go smoothly, follow these tips:

- Have a cash float filled with coins and small bills. All yard sales are cash only and most people retrieve their cash from bank machines these days, which means that most people will hand you a 20-dollar bill when they make a purchase. Use an apron with pockets so you can keep the cash handy at all times for a quick sale.

- Have several old sheets, shower curtains, tarps, or other "drop sheets" in the mix so that you can quickly set one down on the lawn (which might be damp) or the driveway (which may be dirty) and have a protective area to load the goods onto. They will also come in handy if you have items in the same space (such as tools in your garage) that aren't for sale.

- Be realistic about your prices and let people know that you'll give them discounts if they buy several items. You're holding a garage sale, not an antiques auction. If you have items of significant value, it's unlikely you'll get their worth at a garage sale, so consider putting them away and selling them via a different channel.

- Sometimes people can be very, very cheap. Bartering is a part of the yard sale mentality and can be a part of its fun too, but that doesn't mean that your items or pricing should be disrespected. An item that you bought for 100 dollars and used once or twice may be valued at 20 dollars at your sale. If someone offers you 15 dollars, that's a pretty good deal. Remember, if you're hoping to recoup much of the original purchase price of any item, a garage sale is not the place to be selling it.

- During your sale, do your best to keep things neat. For example, if you're selling books, don't just toss them all in a crate. Your customers will not take the time to dig through a big mess of books to see if there's one they might like. Instead, display them on a shelf with their spines out so that people can easily browse through the titles. The more user-friendly and attractive your displays, the more items you'll sell. Putting a little bit of effort into the presentation adds further value to your items; there is a psychological impact to making everything look nice and more perceived value equals more money for you.

- Put on your best customer service face. Yes, it's "just" a garage sale, but a sour salesperson will deter your customers. Make eye contact with everyone who stops to look at your items and answer questions as politely as possible. I sold in the markets for many years and was astonished at how many people went to the trouble of bringing all their wares to the market and then talked on their mobile phones all day with their backs to the customers. At the end of the day they had to take it all home again because they had turned off virtually every potential buyer who stopped by. Offer the best customer service you can and you will be rewarded with more items gone at the end of the day and more cash in hand.
- Get a helper or two. Not only will this help you catch all the customers, but it will also help you keep a better eye on things. Unfortunately, people do steal things from garage sales. The more pairs of eyes you have, the better.
- Have a "FREE" bin. You may have items with no real value but that you're still reluctant to throw away. You'd be surprised how people will gladly take

picture frames with the glass missing, torn books, old craft supplies... just because it's junk to you doesn't mean it's junk to everyone. Put your "FREE" bin at the front of your sale to attract more passersby.

Tip #13: Making Even More at Your Garage Sale

Want to earn even more money at your garage sale? Sell coffee, bottled water, homemade cookies, etc. Again, put these items near the front of your sale where they will entice not only the people walking by, but also the customers who are already browsing through your items. Selling treats is great because it caters to people's tendencies to impulse-buy. This can work great later in the day, when sales tend to droop but people are getting hungry and need a little something to tide them over till the evening.

And just like I was talking about earlier, if you have a good reason for holding your garage sale, make a big poster to let people know. You'll be amazed at how much more generous people are when they know you're having the sale to help pay down some debt, save up for your children's education, or even fix your car. If you can strike a personal chord with your customers, you'll definitely make more sales.

Tip #14: Clear Out Old Stock

There are a lot of people out there who just can't resist a bargain, so why not appeal to them and make some extra cash at the same time? If you own or have owned a business, there may be old or surplus stock that you can put on sale at temptingly low prices. When I owned retail shops, I discovered that reducing the prices on old stock by only 20 percent usually got the job done. Suddenly, items that had been ignored for months were flying right out of the bargain baskets and into customers' hands.

If you've got an existing business, try putting a sale rack at the front door so that people will spot your items before they even set foot in the store. If you don't have your business anymore or you just haven't got a retail outlet, rent a spot in one of your local markets to sell your items. Either way, you'll be glad you did something about all that extra stuff - not only will this idea generate you some cash quickly, but it will also get rid of old stock that was just sitting around taking up valuable space.

If you do have a business, here's another benefit of putting your old stock on sale and it may just be the boost your business has been craving: by placing inexpensive items right at your front door where people can see them, it will attract customers into your store whether they decide to buy your sale items or not. If they perceive your store as one that offers good value, they will be enticed to come in and shop around. Once they are inside, they will be more likely to make other purchases, which of course will increase your sales. Even if they buy nothing at all, once they have been inside, chances greatly increase that they will come back again looking for other bargains. This is especially true if you sell specialty items in your shop.

This technique is so effective that many businesses deliberately choose to sell some stock at near cost or even at a loss to bring extra customers through the doors. These items are commonly known as "loss leaders" and using them is a wonderful strategy to draw in those people who otherwise may not have been enticed into your shop. Try it out if you're looking for a way to seriously increase the number of people coming through your doors.

Remember that the main reason items don't sell is because people don't want them badly enough for the price you're asking. When this happens, it is often because an entrepreneur hasn't done sufficient market research before spending precious capital on acquiring the inventory in question.

Tip #15: Sell for Less Than Cost When You Must

My friend Nancy was fiercely involved with cancer advocacy and created some excellent products around the issues that she so passionately wrote and performed about. Unfortunately, she didn't conduct her market research before she spent a lot of time and money developing, creating, and producing these products. They are brilliant and beautiful - but they are also collecting dust in her spare room! Needless to say, she has learned her lesson and will never make this mistake again.

But what she does have now, aside from newfound wisdom, is inventory. She knows that she needs to get creative and find places where she can sell her wares. Even if she sells for less than cost she will still get some cash in hand and will probably make a positive difference to the people who end up with her products, which were designed to empower those touched by cancer.

Keep Nancy's story in mind if you have excess inventory of your own. Although I'm sure you'd love to make loads of money off of your items, selling them at a loss may be your best bet if they genuinely don't have worth to consumers. The upside is you'll get quick cash and hopefully recover some space in your home, which could be put to more productive and profitable uses. For example, if your basement, spare bedroom, or garage is full of old business stuff, clearing it out could make space to rent out as storage or living space.

Tip #16: Change Your Spending Habits

If you're strapped for cash, good news: you might actually have the money you need to get by without even knowing it. Sometimes all you have to do is take a look at where your money is going and change the habits that are money wasters. The financial worksheets that you completed earlier in this book were probably an eye-opener for you! This is the time to retrieve your list of expenses and check back in with your pared-down, more realistic budget.

Fortunately, budgets can continue to be tweaked as needed. If you need cash for a one-off expense like a new suit for job-hunting or to get your business started, take a look at your daily activities and see if you can temporarily cut out whatever is costing a lot. For example, maybe you could take the bus to work for a while. It may not be as convenient as your car, but a monthly bus pass is much easier on the wallet than fuel, parking, and maintenance bills. (If you do consider this option, talk to your insurance company about suspending your coverage until you start driving again - this could be a big money saver as well.)

If you've got longer-term money troubles, get serious and start thinking about what you could truly do without for a good long while. Perhaps you could forego going out for drinks or dinner with your friends. Restaurants and bars are so expensive and you can often have a much nicer time if you stay in. You could invite your friends over for a potluck dinner or throw a party where everyone brings a bottle of their favorite wine. It can be a lot of fun to mix your own drinks or make a yummy punch, rather than overpaying at a crowded bar. Check the Internet for hundreds of delicious ideas. I for one have thrown many fantastic parties by having everyone bring something to eat, something to drink, and their favorite CDs to play.

Either way, it's helpful to sit down with a pen, paper, and calculator for this activity. Ask yourself if each expense is a necessity or a luxury. For some habits, you'll need to be really ruthless to figure out which is which. Remember, you must be honest if you want to make any progress. Your goal is to find out how much the things you do are actually costing you, and which of those things can be cut out of your life, at least temporarily.

Another reason for writing it down is that it can be easier to prioritize your spending habits if you see them on paper in front of you. You may be surprised to discover where your money is actually going. Think about it: if you spend only two unnecessary dollars a day, that's 60 dollars at the end of the month that could have paid your mobile phone bill or your life insurance premium. In that light, it will be harder for you to let slide that 10-dollar daily coffee-and-dessert habit or the costly cable television package. When reality is staring back at you from a piece of paper, it will be easier for you to figure out which habits can stay and which ones need to go.

Ideally, the trick to bringing more cash into your life is to increase your earnings, but decreasing your spending is also a great way to find that emergency money you need, get those bills paid, or pay down some costly credit card debt. You'll be surprised at how much of that end-of-the-month stress you can alleviate by being a little more vigilant over your spending.

Tip #17: What Are Your Treats Really Costing You?

Don't get me wrong - it's nice to treat yourself. However, when you don't have enough to make ends meet, those short-term, costly gratifications can be doing significantly more harm than good. Not only are you spending money you don't really have on things you don't really need, you're also creating additional stress for yourself in a situation that is already stressful enough.

What is it costing you to go to the hairdresser as often as you do? Couldn't you be saving quite a bit of money by coloring your hair at home? What about expensive gym memberships, new shoes, and manicures? Don't forget eating out when you just don't feel like cooking. Those restaurant dates add up, especially if you're ordering a bottle of wine or two or, other than tap water, any beverage at all.

By following some of the advice in this book, you'll be able to work out how much your treats are really costing you and which of them are expendable. It isn't easy to make these sacrifices, but think of all the people who are surviving on even less. Think about how much smarter you could be with that money. Think about what it will be like to finally be debt-free with a steady, reliable cash flow to support you.

To help you along, allow yourself to dream about the future. What do you want it to look like? What will it take to get you there? How are your little short-term treats affecting those big long-term goals? Are they costing you the deposit on a home of your own? Are they costing you the education that would get you the job of your dreams? Are they costing you the life you want to give your children? By dreaming about the future, you'll get a fresh perspective on the present. Once you've got your dreams firmly in mind, don't let anything get in the way of them, including unnecessary spending.

Tip #18: Treating Yourself - The Smart Way

While you're working on cutting out costly goods and services you simply don't need, focus on rewarding yourself with free treats instead of expensive ones. You don't need to deprive yourself, you just need to shift your concept of reward.

Have a bubble bath, watch a movie from the library, call a friend for a chat, throw a board game party, or go for a walk in the park. There are plenty of ways to have fun and relax without spending money; all it takes is a little imagination.

If you're having trouble restricting yourself, a great trick is to make a deal with yourself or, better yet, someone in your support network. Set some boundaries. Even my five-year-old niece understands that every time we have an outing she is allowed one treat. If she wants french fries, I remind her that she can choose that, but that choice means that there will be no other treats for the remainder of the day. If we walk around the corner and an ice cream truck is waiting there, she may want one of those too, but she has learned (remarkably quickly I might add) that I am firm and serious on this rule. She has also learned to savor her choices and when she finally settles on her one and only treat she gets so much pleasure out of it that I find it a real pleasure to watch!

Why can't we, as adults, put this kind of boundary around our own treats? The answer is that we can, but when we have the autonomy to act on each and every impulse, things can become tricky. Nevertheless, I encourage you to try to make it fun for yourself, as it has become for my niece. Perhaps you'd love that latte right now, but wouldn't a glass of wine after work also be nice? By choosing only one, you'll build some anticipation, save some money, and fuel your momentum towards the bigger goal of a wealthy life free from financial burden.

Remember that once you're free and clear of your money problems, the cash that was going toward expensive debt or other wasteful things can instead be put towards nice things like savings and luxury items. Once you've gotten rid of your financial worries and can afford the occasional treat, you'll actually enjoy them much more because you'll know that they aren't harming your financial situation or your future.

Tip #19: Use Schools and Training Centers

My friend Meg made a huge find one day while she was walking around town. She saw the sign "Hairdressing Academy" and took note of the name. Once home, she phoned them and asked some questions.

At first glance, she thought she would never get her precious (and gorgeous) locks cut, colored, or styled by anyone who wasn't properly trained and experienced. So she was happily surprised to learn that all of the students were already trained and experienced hairdressers; they were simply back in training for new products that this one particular chain was launching.

She also learned that there were different levels of students at the academy. The new students, who were trained hairdressers but new to the academy, offered the lowest rates. The only caveat with these students was that the appointments were longer than average because everything that the student was doing had to be carefully checked by an instructor (which would give nervous new customers like my friend Meg some serious peace of mind!).

The second tier of students charged slightly higher rates and the graduate students charged the most, but even the highest-paid students there charged well below the market value of their services. Meg decided to use a graduate student to revitalize her color and a new student to trim her simple haircut.

Are there any hairdressing schools in your town where you can get your hair done for less? Since Meg's first visit, about seven years ago, she has averaged about five color treatments and six haircuts per year (a conservative amount by many standards). The salon she used previously charged about 150 dollars (tax and tip included) per highlighting appointment and 80 dollars per haircut. At five visits per year the total would be 750 dollars for the highlights and 480 dollars for the haircuts, for a grand total of 1,230 dollars each and every year... and that doesn't include shampoos, conditioners, hair products, and styling equipment!

By contrast, she now spends about 70 dollars per highlighting appointment, or 350 dollars per year. Her haircuts are about 20 dollars per visit or 120 dollars per year. Her total overall cost at the hairdressing academy is just 470 dollars, which gives her an overall savings of roughly 760 dollars

- about 60 percent. The number of mishaps she has had in these seven years totals two: both of which were fixed quickly, graciously, apologetically, and at no charge. Does your regular salon offer that kind of service?

You can apply this money-saving trick to all kinds of scenarios. A beauty school may offer cut-rate appointments for waxing, manicures, pedicures, eyebrow threading, massages, facials, etc. If you need to hire a caterer, a band, or a photographer for an event such as a wedding or family party, check out cooking and art colleges to see who's willing to do the work inexpensively in exchange for the experience.

You might need a little extra patience and time for students, but in most cases, the money you'll save will be well worth the additional time. A quick flip through the phone book or an online search will likely turn up a few great options in your area.

Tip #20: Get Rid of Magazines and Newspapers

Face it: your subscriptions, no matter what they are, are a luxury item. Aside from all the extra work they generate (you have to read them, stack them, recycle them...), they are available for free in many places. Consider reading your favorite publications online or at the library, your local coffee shop, or even at the hairdresser. Also, for magazines, keep and eye out at local yard sales and in your neighborhood recycling bins.

Thanks to the Internet and television, reading your newspaper isn't really necessary anymore to get your news fix. Sure, it's nice to get the newspaper delivered to your front door and peruse it over your morning cup of coffee, but when you're facing serious financial issues, it's worth the money you'll save to get your news in a different way.

Most publications have excellent websites that show much of the same content found in their print versions for free. Or, if you're already paying for cable anyway, why not watch your news on television with loved ones?

Many newspapers and magazines now also offer subscriptions to their online content, so you can get access to the exact content you'd find in their print publications, plus videos, polls, bonus articles, interactive forums, and other additional content. These subscriptions often cost less than the print versions, so if you simply can't do away with your subscription addiction, at least choose one that is more affordable.

Tip #21: "Freegans"

I'm not suggesting that you become a dumpster-diver, but it is always wise to keep your eyes open. People throw perfectly good things away, things that could easily have a longer life.

There is a new movement that I recently learned about on the news. The people who belong to this movement call themselves "freegans" and they pride themselves on avoiding the consumer-driven lifestyle. Although many of these people are educated as well as successful in the world, they are so angry at the sheer amount of waste that our society creates that they do everything they can to not spend money.

There are tons, literally tons, of perfectly unspoiled, sealed packages of food that go into grocery store dumpsters on a regular basis. There are places in New York City where the freegans gather every week to collect the produce and other groceries that were otherwise destined for the dumpsters. They walk away with shrink-wrapped packages of corn on the cob, salad, fruit, dairy products, cheese, muffins, bread, and more.

What I was most shocked by was that these products were being thrown away en masse not because they had reached their "best before" dates, although this is sometimes the case. In many cases, each store simply assigns a time of the week when the massive discard happens. This waste is simply standard operating procedure!

If waiting for discarded food feels a bit extreme to you, you can still adopt the freegan lifestyle in other ways. For example, if you could use some new furniture, check the "free" categories in your local online classified ad site. I was amazed at the kinds of things people are giving away - from living room furniture to dining sets to televisions and more! These sites are also great for new or expecting moms; there are lots of listings for baby clothing, furniture, and toys.

You can also use these free categories if there are things you would otherwise have to pay to get rid of. For example, if you would have to pay someone or rent a truck to get rid of old rusty appliances in your garage, post your need instead. Two newlywed friends of mine purchased an old house with lots of non-working appliances and light fixtures and got rid of them all for free by simply posting a Craigslist ad.

What other ways could you add freegan elements into your own lifestyle? Get creative and involve your family. Shopaholics out there might be surprised to find that the rush of getting something for nothing is even better than finding something on sale!

Chapter 3: Make the Most of Your Resources

Earlier in the book, I talked about your resources. Your resources may be easy or difficult to spot, depending on your general level of self-confidence as well as the degree to which you're worried about money.

The more centered and present you are, the easier it will be for you to spot your resources. Utilizing your resources is all about taking what you have and using it in a way that creates even more. The goal is financial freedom and a true sense of abundance - and everyone truly can make it happen simply by using the resources they have at their disposal.

Believe in yourself and let's get going - it's time to find and leverage those amazing resources of yours so you can enjoy the fullest expression of wealth that this life has to offer.

Tip #22: Compounding Can Make All the Difference

If you are not generating enough income right now, you need to ask yourself what isn't working. Earlier I was talking about the importance of interest rates. Let's look into that a little further now.

Do you want to spend your time receiving interest or paying it? Whether you're good at saving money or not, it's in your best interests to learn how to make the money you do have work for you so that you don't have to work for your money later on. If you don't know about the miracle of compound interest, it's time to get educated. Compound interest can make a huge difference to your finances over the length of your life.

If you were to stuff 100 dollars under your mattress each year, 25 years later you'd have saved 2,500 dollars. Now, not only is 2,500 dollars not a whole lot of money in the grand scheme of things, but 25 years down the road, it's going to be worth even less. Why? One reason: the time value of money, which is a fancy financial term that simply means that inflation is going to eat away at your savings year after year unless you earn more interest than the rate of inflation. The rising cost of living means that as time goes by, it takes more money to buy the same things. Remember how much less expensive things used to be when you were a kid? Maybe your grandparents used to tell you how "in the old days" everything used to cost much less. It's the same principle: the 2,500 dollars you've saved won't buy you as much later on as it does today, unless you do something about it.

Now, let's say you put that 100 dollars a year into a savings account or investment that pays an average of 10 percent compound interest. Compound interest means that any interest you earn gets rolled into your initial deposit amount, so that you earn interest on the interest, too. If you invest your 100 dollars a year into a compound interest account, you'll get quite a different result. After 25 years, your 2,500-dollar investment would be worth about 10,000 dollars.

This result only gets better when you increase the time, percentage yield, and/or amount of principal you put in. For instance, if you put in 10,000 dollars instead of 100 dollars each year into an account that compounds daily, the final amount is more like 1.24 *million* dollars after 25 years. Pretty exciting, isn't it? The best part of all is that these dramatic figures are not at all unrealistic once you've got your money out from under your mattress and into the right account.

To choose the best account or investment for you, get informed by speaking with a financial advisor. Ask if the interest is calculated daily or monthly; this will make a big difference over time. Also, definitely investigate any investments you're interested in very carefully. Ask about all the associated risks and how you can protect yourself against those risks. Ask for your responses in writing, if possible, so that you can read over them in your own time and have a record for review purposes (email correspondence is great for record keeping). Of course, make sure you choose one with a growth rate greater than the rate of inflation, so you can be sure that your money will be there to support you in the future. The greater the difference between the rate of inflation and the growth rate of your investment, the faster your money will grow.

There are lots of fun compounding calculators on the Internet these days. Just type “compound interest calculator” into a search engine and play with the numbers!

Tip #23: Get Educated About Your Taxes

In Australia, like in every developed country in the world, we have a very complex taxation system. There are so many tricky rules and so many ins and outs to know that a lot of people find it easier to just give everything to someone else - anyone else - to take care of it for them. When it’s time to pay taxes or send in monthly statements, they just can’t be bothered with the stress and confusion of figuring it all out for themselves, so they give up and let someone else do it.

I’m here to tell you, don’t give up! For most of us, it’s worth taking the time to understand how the tax system can help us as business owners, investors, or even as parents. There is no one you can hire who will have as vested an interest in your personal and business finances as you. Most of the time, it’s better for you to take the initiative to get educated so that you understand precisely when and why you owe money and when and why you don’t.

If your area has a taxpayers' organization, I strongly recommend joining it. These organizations dedicate themselves to helping taxpayers understand the system they are paying into. They usually have a number of publications all designed to help you learn everything you need to know about preparing for and paying your taxes. It may seem like a lot of work, but investing the time into teaching yourself about the system can only benefit you and may end up saving you a lot of money in the long run.

Again, a good financial advisor or accountant will be able to help you structure your finances to work within the system for best effect. Take the time to meet with several professionals before deciding whom you'd prefer to work with. Choose somebody who listens to you, understands your personal and professional goals, and has enough experience in the system to really give you your money's worth. Don't be shy about asking for references; a good advisor or accountant will be more than happy to pass along contact information from his or her past clients so you can judge for yourself how good his or her service is likely to be. Remember, it's not just about finding someone with the proper credentials; it's also about finding the person who will be the best fit for you and your goals.

For most of us, the thought of devoting a significant amount of time to learning about the taxation system is quite unappealing. However, let's look at the importance of it from another perspective: imagine the taxation system as your partner. Sound crazy? Well, this partner is going to be taking its share of your earnings to pay for its portion of your partnership. In many cases, this amounts to nearly a 50/50 split of your earnings. Wouldn't it be in your best interests to understand how your partner works and how your earnings are to be divided among the two of you? Even if you don't like the comparison, know that as you grow in both business and personal financial success, you'll be glad that you took the time to get to know your taxation system.

Tip #24: Do a Lost Money Search

When you're short on cash, it may seem unbelievable that people have money in the bank that they've actually forgotten about, but it really does happen. Check with your tax office to see if you have any "lost" money in super funds. You can also simply type "Lost Super" into a search engine to find lots of websites you can use to check if you have any unclaimed super sitting in an account that you have lost track of. In Australia, the ASIC website will also help you find lost bank accounts and such. To use their services, just go to www.MoneySmart.gov.au. I personally was amazed at the amounts of money that people have not claimed. (At the time of writing, the Money Smart website also maintains a database of complaints about financial advisors and institutions, handy advice about scams, managing money, borrowing, and investing.)

Check to see what similar services are available in your area and be diligent about it. Wouldn't it be wonderful to uncover some old, forgotten money that could help alleviate some of your current financial burden?

When it comes to missing money, don't forget to check your bank accounts! I meet a lot of people who have small amounts of cash spread between lots of bank accounts. This situation can cost a lot of money not only because it's easy to lose track of so many accounts, but also because it can reduce the amount of interest you earn overall and cost more in fees to maintain. If you are one of these people with too many accounts, you are probably paying much more than you have to in bank fees. You also could be getting a better return on your cash if you used it to pay off bad debt or combined it all into a higher interest account with just one institution. In any case, it's in your best interests to find all those accounts; you might just stumble on some money to help you through the tough times.

Tip #25: Other Places to Search for Lost Money

When is the last time you checked the back of your sock drawer, your "secret hiding spot," or under the mattress for hidden money? Okay, so you might only end up digging a bit of change out of your sofa cushions but remember, it all adds up. Go through your jackets, old pants pockets, last year's handbags, the luggage you used on your last holiday... these items have a way of hiding money from you for months or even years. Sure, it's maybe not a ton of cash, but what good is it doing you in some old forgotten pocket? One of my friends tosses all his loose change in a bowl. One day he counted it and found there was enough to buy an airline ticket to the other side of the world!

How about all those notebooks, envelopes, and file folders where you have stashed gift cards or gift certificates? Are you sure that you have used them all up? It's worth a double check. Even if you don't need that particular product or service right now, you may be able to barter with it to gain something of real value to you.

Pursue any and all avenues you can imagine towards reclaiming money. Be open to opportunity along the way. Finding more money and making more money is a journey like any other in life. It's best if you can relax into it a bit; be easy and light about it. That attitude really helps the opportunities flow and gives you the ability to see them and to seize them.

Tip #26: Do You Have Any International Currency?

Foreign exchange is something of an art and a science combined. It fascinates me both as an investor and as someone with an interest in what is going on in the rest of the world. Foreign currency investment is not without its risks, however. It is not something to get involved with unless you have a passion for it, a solid education in it, and a pot of money to work with.

If that doesn't describe you, don't worry - you're in good company. Luckily, you might still be able to make something bigger of any international currencies you have, so take a look and see what you have. Perhaps you have some money kicking around from your last foreign holiday. Cash leftover in a currency you don't normally use often goes unused and unnoticed until your next vacation. Instead of letting it go to waste in your travel wallet, collect it together and organize it. Then, get online to find the local currency exchange. These outlets usually offer a better exchange rate than any bank will offer. They are likely to have a website that is updated several times a day in order to keep you on top of the ever-changing currency rates.

These sites are also a very valuable resource for other relevant links such as companies that track and chart currencies. They usually offer charts and graphs that offer you a great visual to track any world currencies, which is a good way to get to know the trends.

A basic understanding of currency trends will help you in deciding what the best time will be to cash in these currencies at a tidy profit. Hey, it may not amount to much, but isn't it better to put it into a currency you can use than do nothing with it at all?

Tip #27: Do You Have Any Collectibles?

It is remarkable what some people collect. Basically, there are as many categories of collectibles as there are categories of personality types and these objects are very dear to the hearts of those who collect them. Antique bottles or decanters, vintage dolls and Barbies, all things Avon, Swarovski crystal ornaments, train sets, stamps, collector sets of coins, Royal Doulton figurines, fine china and pottery, first edition books or signed copies of books, fine wine vintages, comic books, hockey cards, action figures, vintage toys...The list is nearly endless.

Are there any items that you have in your home or in storage that may possibly have value to others? Think about it and keep your mind open when reviewing your items. Anything that may possibly be a collectible is worth an online search to investigate. There are websites for just about every hobby, interest, and collectible imaginable and most of these provide very detailed information. Internet searches are quick, easy, and free, so it should take no time at all to discover whether your trash is someone else's treasure.

This is a potentially lucrative market because people have a sentimental or emotional involvement with the objects they have chosen to collect. It is definitely worth your while to take a mental and physical inventory and see if anything could be sold to a collector. Then get online to assess the value and see what your next step could be.

You could take this idea one step further by bringing your iPad or smart phone with you to garage sales on the hunt for collectibles. Take a look through what's in someone's yard sale and, if you see something that might be of value, take a look online to "guesstimate" what you could potentially sell it for. Often people are getting rid of antique furniture or other extremely valuable items for next to nothing at garage sales because they are unaware of their value and/or simply trying to declutter their homes. You never know when you might stumble across a hidden treasure!

Tip #28: Hire Yourself Out as a Contractor or Consultant

Everyone is good at something. Is there a service you could perform and sell? There are literally thousands of people looking for unique skills like yours every single day of the week. They need everything from artists to writers to cleaners to computer-savvy people; I promise you the demand is virtually endless.

I have a friend who was stretched thin from the Christmas money crunch, student loan payments, and the fact that she'd been unemployed for two months. She decided to see if she could somehow make some money writing (she does have a degree in English - hence the student loan woes) until she found full-time work. Well, after not even two weeks, she had done writing jobs for a real estate agent and an online article company, and she had landed a weekly article-writing job. Three weeks after that, she landed writing contracts for two big websites. Two weeks after that, her first e-book deal was signed. What was meant to be a temporary fix to get her through a rough time turned into full-time work in only a matter of weeks.

So, how did she tap into all this unmet demand? The Internet!

The Internet has absolutely revolutionized the way buyers and sellers connect. It has changed the business environment in a manner that allows you to make money simply by having a computer, an Internet connection, and a marketable skill.

Not sure if you have a marketable skill or not? I'm willing to wager that you do. Sit down for a moment and think about the life experiences you've had that would be of benefit to others. You don't have to have actual job experience in order to have a marketable skill. Perhaps you could sell your crafts, your closet organization techniques, your green thumb...

Chances are, the Internet can help you find customers who've been waiting for skills just like yours. There are dozens of great websites that have been created for the express purpose of linking buyers and service providers together. Take a look at sites such as Elance.com, Rentacoder.com, IFreelance.com, and Freelancer.com. Also check out Etsy, Craigslist, Gumtree, Trading Post, and any other local websites in your area that help connect the people within your community. These are all great websites that get a lot of hits every day, so you can be sure that people are going to see what you have to offer.

Nearly all of these websites post new projects every day needing writers, artists, programmers, various technical experts, administrative assistance, engineers... the list goes on and on and on. Some of these websites are free to join, but take a small percentage of your earnings; others charge a small monthly fee and let you keep all of the earnings for yourself. Still others are free altogether. Shop around to find the website that's right for you.

If you start earning a lot, you may need to check with your local tax office to ensure that you are complying with their reporting standards. I have always found them to be very helpful, but I do recommend that you communicate with the tax office and all financial advisors in writing. This helps to ensure that you are clear on all of the details, avoid miscommunications, and create a paper trail in case there are any issues or disputes down the road.

Another fantastic way to market your skills is to set up a website of your own. That way you can build an online portfolio, showcase pictures of your work, list your client testimonials, keep people updated with a blog, and more. A website isn't necessary to get started, but will definitely prove helpful down the road. As your new business gains popularity, a website will allow potential new clients to find you instead of you having to seek them out.

Don't get overwhelmed about your website just yet. Remember, they aren't necessary to get started. Just take it one step at a time: choose one of your skills to market and start from there.

Tip #29: Turn Your Ideas Into E-Books

Transform your interests and expertise into a marketable product by creating an e-book that you can sell on the Internet. E-books are fantastic because they don't require any elaborate business setup and you don't need to bother with publishing or distribution costs. You don't even have to do the writing yourself. The websites I mentioned above are great for finding experienced and enthusiastic writers to put your great ideas into print form, often at very reasonable rates.

To market your e-book, you will either need to use a readymade service such as CreateSpace, which allows you to sell your e-books on Amazon, or you will need a website and a PayPal account. On the website, include positive reviews, enticing snippets from the e-book, and the top few reasons a person should purchase your e-book. Next, you'll need a way to receive money - that's where the PayPal account comes in. PayPal is an ingenious company set up to help ordinary people send and receive funds over the Internet. It's free to have an account; PayPal only takes a small percentage of the funds that you receive.

Another great marketing idea is to simply email your friends and family about your new e-book and ask them to pass along your website address to anyone they know who might be interested. It's better to involve people who know and respect you than to do a costly mass emailing scheme that will only land your messages in people's junk mail folders.

If you already have a writing portfolio, be sure to showcase it on your website and in your emails so that you can establish some credibility. It's also a good idea to start a blog to generate interest in your ideas and your e-book. Do a search online for "how to market blogs" for pointers on how to get up and running using your blog as a promotional tool for your e-book.

An e-book may not bring in a lot of money at first, but the exposure will bring in customers whose testimonials you can use to promote that e-book and others in the future. Gradually, interest in your e-book(s) will snowball until one day you may have an Internet business that virtually runs itself, requiring you to do almost nothing except collect the cash.

The key is to consider making the most of what you already have in that fabulous brain of yours! Not only can an e-book earn you money, but it also is wonderful for helping you establish credibility on whatever subject you choose for your e-book. For example, if you write an e-book about how to perform basic maintenance on your vehicle, you can use your e-book to help market your skills as an auto mechanic. Then, if and when you choose to sell your services, you can tell customers that you are a published author, which will help consumers build confidence in your business. Once you publish subsequent books, you'll be able to market them to that same client base, which means ongoing income from your e-books as well as an increasingly loyal customer group.

Tip #30: Become a Personal or Business Coach

Once again, we're going to take a look at your skill set as an untapped source of income. Think of the things that you're good at or interested in - more than likely, many of these are skills that other people would love to improve upon in their own lives. For example, do you have superior organizational skills or fabulous de-stressing techniques? Are you a born salesperson? These are all things that can put money in your pocket when offered as coaching services to the right people.

It may seem obvious, but if you are offering your services to friends or colleagues, make it clear that you will expect them to pay you for your time or make an exchange for something of equal value. I find that no matter how good your advice is, many people will not value it appropriately if it has been given too freely. Therefore, decide what you need as compensation for your services and make your needs plain in advance of providing the coaching. You may ask for a flat rate, charge an hourly fee, or perhaps trade coaching sessions (coaching in your area of expertise in exchange for coaching in theirs). Just make sure you feel that you are being remunerated fairly.

It can be tricky getting started because sometimes you'll identify an area someone needs help in before he or she does. In this case, you may want to gently point out how you could assist them, but it's best to let them come to you for help. It has been my experience that just because you think you can help someone doesn't mean that they are ready or willing to receive - much less pay for - your advice.

For those people who are ready and willing, however, often all they need is a little direction to improve an area of their life. You could help them by identifying some milestones to achieve on their path to improvement and then setting up a regular schedule to assist them in meeting those goals. Much of what makes an effective coach is simply being there to help your clients stay on track and keep clear about the goals that you have helped them set for themselves. A weekly or bi-weekly schedule is great for your clients because it helps them plan their progress and track their success. It's also great for you, the coach, because it means both an easier time charting your clients' progress and, of course, a steady stream of compensation.

Nowadays there are a lot of companies and educational institutions offering training to become a life coach or a business coach. With stress and depression currently being major problems in developed countries, it's no surprise that well-qualified coaches are in high demand. However, before changing careers, investing in this type of education, or buying an expensive coaching franchise, do some serious research about the potential of the business in your area and whether it's the right fit for you. Depending on local demand and your individual needs, it may be best to stick to a more casual coaching routine.

If you decide that you are serious about coaching, then do some research into the best educational programs to help you along your new career path. I personally have had greater success in my life since studying NLP (Neurolinguistic Programming). NLP has made me a much better coach and communicator. I highly recommend finding a good course on the subject or reading books about it.

Tip #31: Become a Tutor

Are you strong in mathematics or any languages? Do you have a knack for explaining things to people? If so, you may find it's actually quite simple to pick up some extra income by tutoring.

Advertise your services using leaflets and advertisements in school newspapers and on notice boards. Colleges and universities are great places to start - students are always looking for tutors on virtually every subject imaginable. Also, if you know any teachers or parents, let them know what your skills are and that you are available for tutoring. Parents and teachers are constantly looking for someone trustworthy to help their kids, so your personal reputation with them can go a long way in securing a bit of regular business. It's also always a good idea to offer referral bonuses to your customers so that they are encouraged to pass along your name to others.

Another great tip is to try international schools because often those parents and/or their children are in need of language tutoring, skill set updating, or just general cultural acclimatization. Also, families attending international schools are in many cases involved with a larger community of foreigners, all of whom may be in need of tutoring or coaching services. If you can impress just one person in that network, you may have a generous amount of referral business coming your way.

Don't overlook the possibility of doing this work online. Today there is a lot of great meeting, conferencing and video-calling software that makes meeting in cyberspace inexpensive and simple. My friend's niece received math tutoring all throughout high school via Skype. This technology can expand your opportunities, so let your imagination go there!

Tip #32: Get Referral Fees for Helping Others

If you know of a great service or product provider that you would be happy to recommend to your friends and people you meet, talk to that provider about setting up a referral arrangement. You'd be surprised what people will be willing to give you if only you ask. This way you can earn a fee or free products when someone you refer spends money with that company.

I know many people who take advantage of these opportunities by hosting parties that showcase kitchen products, cosmetics, jewelry, or unique clothing lines. Not only do they get incentives for simply holding these parties in their homes, they also get additional compensation relative to how much product their friends buy. It's a simple way to earn money for telling people about products and services you truly believe in.

You could even take this idea in a new direction by setting up your own business evaluating service providers in an area that interests you and report on your findings through a subscription service. Subscribers would pay a fee to purchase your report, which would contain plenty of helpful consumer information. As your subscription base grew, so would your cash flow, with very little additional work involved.

For instance, you could price out 100 popular items at 10 local supermarkets and prepare a report about your findings showing the differences in the prices, how enjoyable the shopping experience was at each store, etc. Then advertise your report through the local media. You could also ask the most competitive shops in the report for an additional discount for your customers, which may be redeemed by a coupon from your report. Then you could perhaps ask for a commission on the additional sales generated by your report. You could also make extra money by having other nearby businesses (in industries other than those in your report) place advertisements in your report.

Did you notice that once we got rolling with this idea, it just got bigger and bigger? How much further could it go? There are many variations on this theme - just do a bit of brainstorming on your own or with friends to find one that works for you. As you can see, creative thinking truly is key to getting out of your money crisis. Remember to focus on your ultimate goal with this tip, which is helping people. Let the money flow naturally from there.

Tip #33: Find Brokers to Pay You for Bringing in Business

Talk to local mortgage, finance, insurance, and real estate brokers to find the ones who are willing to pay you referral fees or give you a percentage of their commissions (under "loan introducer" status) every time you send them new business that earns them additional revenue.

My friend Stella has used this strategy so successfully that she ended up deciding to get her own license, became a mobile lender herself, and now pays others commissions to bring her business. The income generated from making referrals bought her an investment property and will soon be buying her a beautiful new home. I'm so pleased for her!

When you're struggling to make ends meet, stories like Stella's can seem too good to be true, but a positive outlook despite your challenging circumstances may be the motivation you need to follow in her footsteps. It really isn't more complicated than making a few phone calls to find out who will do business with you and then choosing the reputable ones that you feel comfortable recommending to your friends, family, and colleagues.

Tip #34: Help Businesses and People Get Back on Track

Many businesses these days have cash flow problems or are struggling to find the cash to expand their businesses to make them more efficient or profitable. If you can find a lender or leasing agent who will buy those businesses' equipment from them and then lease it back to them, this can provide much needed cash flow. Set up a referral arrangement and then tell everyone you think it would benefit and set up the introductions. I funded my first two businesses this exact way, by borrowing the money using the equipment as collateral and then leasing it back on a monthly basis. The leasing payment was a legitimate business expense - and having the cash working to help me grow the business made good sense.

Recently I have helped people find lenders to finance their educational training programs and debt consolidations. Often these lenders have a referral commission structure and you can help your clients by doing the research to find out who are the more reputable lenders. A word of caution, however: be aware that just about anything these days where you are advising people on their finances can put you in danger of being under legal obligations of duty of care over your clients' actions and outcomes. Talk to your local body of authority over your area's financial advisors and any relevant government body, such as the tax authority, to find out if you need licenses or special agreements and disclaimers. It's better to be safe than sorry; you want to help people, not get them into unnecessary debt that doesn't serve them or the lender.

Tip #35: Barter or Trade Services Whenever You Can

You've been sweating over how to make ends meet. You've been worried that the money in the bank will run out before your next paycheck arrives. It's an agonizingly stressful situation that I can sympathize with entirely.

However, what if I told you that you don't need cash as often as you think? It's true, as long as you aren't afraid to get those famous creative juices of yours flowing. If you have talents or time (and you must have at least one or the other!), you could be exchanging your skills for products and services from others, instead of paying cash for them.

For instance, there are a multitude of services that most people need at some point, but that can be difficult for them to carry out or a bit too pricey to take to a professional. Whether it's taking care of a domestic chore, providing some help around the office, or caring for someone's children, there are sure to be places for you to step in.

Potential domestic chores include:

- ☐ Cleaning house gutters
- ☐ Helping with yard work or snow shoveling
- ☐ Altering clothing
- ☐ Organizing closets or storage spaces (professional organizers make a lot of money and most people don't want to shell that much out, but they sure do want orderly storage!)
- ☐ Home-cooked meals (there is currently a great need for special menus such as vegan, dairy-free, or gluten-free)
- ☐ Refrigerator cleaning and/or freezer defrosting
- ☐ Laundry help or ironing

Potential business help might be:

- ☐ Helping someone prepare a budget
- ☐ Tidying up the workplace, home office, or sorting out filing systems
- ☐ Creating a business or marketing plan
- ☐ Making attractive signs to bring in more sales
- ☐ Distributing mailbox leaflets to promote someone else's company, products or services
- ☐ Office cleaning

Other ideas might include:

- ☐ Making curtains
- ☐ Babysitting so that parents can focus on getting their work done or having a night out
- ☐ Building shelves
- ☐ Assembling furniture
- ☐ House sitting while a neighbor is away
- ☐ Addressing Christmas cards or wedding invitations
- ☐ Home deliveries or driving service
- ☐ Companionship for shut-ins or the elderly

Maybe you have some unique skills that are valuable and in demand such as:

- ☐ Creating websites
- ☐ Developing graphics for marketing and advertising material

- ☐ Calligraphy skills
- ☐ Furniture refinishing expertise
- ☐ General handyman skills
- ☐ Wedding planning
- ☐ Fitness coaching
- ☐ E-book writing
- ☐ Home staging or interior design

Maybe you own some equipment that could be hired out such as:

- ☐ A carpet steam-cleaner
- ☐ A power washer
- ☐ A sewing machine or serger
- ☐ Quality sound recording equipment
- ☐ Power tools
- ☐ Your vehicle
- ☐ Your washer and dryer
- ☐ Specialty kitchen equipment
- ☐ Lawn mower

These are just a few ideas to get you inspired! I encourage you to think outside the box and get creative with your own individual situation, talents, and experience!

Make up a flyer listing all the jobs you can take off the hands of the people you do business with and the shops you buy from. Make it clear that you will exchange your services for theirs, as well as take cash for your time. Be careful how much you take on, though; you'll probably be finding yourself very busy!

A friend of mine's daughter desperately wanted to take dance lessons, but she simply could not afford the extra monthly expense. She approached the owner of the dance school and explained that she couldn't pay for lessons but wondered if there was some service she could perform to get the lessons at a discounted rate. It turned out that the owner was in need of someone to clean the mirrors and sweep the studio floors a couple of times a week. It also turned out that the owner was already in the habit of making this exact exchange with other families in similar circumstances. It was a perfect situation for everyone because the owner got clean dance studios every day of the week, my friend had something to do while she waited for her daughter to finish her lessons, and of course, my friend's daughter got to fulfill her passion for dance.

Many people don't consider this option simply because they feel embarrassed that they are asking for something for free. Let me assure you that this is not at all the case. If you were to pay someone money for their products or services, they would in turn go out and spend that money on what they need themselves. If you can fill that need personally, there is no need to exchange cash. You're simply eliminating the cash portions of these transactions to avoid either of you having to spend money at all. So don't be shy; just ask!

Also, remember that even though no one's paying cash at this point, your services are worth something substantial. Make sure you value your time and efforts appropriately, or people will be less likely to take you seriously. Of course, you also want to avoid being taken advantage of, especially in times of serious financial difficulty.

You should note that all barter and exchanges may still considered to be taxable income, depending on your specific tax jurisdiction. You may need to keep proper records of all such transactions and include them in your annual tax reporting. Check with either your local tax office or accountant as to your tax liability in this regard.

Tip #36: Expert Insight From Dee Havebond

Mifestyle: How to Start Your Own Business From Scratch Using No Money and Make Profit Within a Week!

Dee Havebond is an energetic and enthusiastic entrepreneur. Dee teaches mums how to build fun, down to earth businesses from home but not limited to home. Dee excels in creating the Ultimate Lifestyle as a mum and a wife so has playfully coined the term "Mifestyle". Her proven business methods are easy to model, duplicatable and can be replicated step by step. Dee's business model can get you started for no cost to low cost and get you profit within a week.

So here's the challenge.

From the get-go this is about all of us. Especially if you identify with what's ahead.

Missed one too many sports carnivals? Getting your friends to pick up the kids? Sending them off to before school care so you can get to work? Sound familiar?

It's like the saying when your kids are in the car..."Are we there yet???"

Children have a great way of leveling the playing field when it comes to their time with you, your obligations as a parent and your obligations as a provider for your family.

The practicalities of juggling a career and an income when you have kids can be challenging to say the least , especially if you want to experience them growing up, not just seeing them grow up.

So you need to think outside of the box. I mean the sea container, I mean the...mmm, what is the biggest thing you can get??

You picking up what I'm putting down?

So here's the solution.

YES, we are there yet.

...make money fast doing what you love. It can be really simple too.

I love real estate as a long term strategy which is no way to make quick money. What I'm about to share is what I call my **bread and butter money.** It allows you to get money coming in the door while you work on your bigger goals.

You can do this too. Find your passion and join the dots. This is what I've done. You can take these ideas and make them your own.

Best of all, I do this with my kids and they LOVE IT.

Here's the roadmap. Just follow it and tweak it for your own purposes.

Plug this in to your GPS. Then press start.

#1 *Identify a skill you have all ready that others want to know about.*

One of my passions is sewing. Yep, good old fashion, material, thread and imagination. For years I did fashion design and had lots of fun making and choreographing fashion shows. Sometimes in front of crowd of 10,000 + people.

#2 *Identify your niche market. Who would benefit the most by learning your skill?*

For me I teach kids from the ages of 5 - 9 the art of sewing. Firstly by handsewing and then introducing them slowly to the machine. My other target market is mums who want to make original clothes for themselves or their kids.

#3 *Find a venue.*

When starting up, find a community centre, library, scout hall or town hall. They are usually run by council and they can be free or have low fees to hire, or you can work out a plan to pay the venue when you get paid by your clients.

I've hired the community library in my local area which serves three components. It supports the local community, it serves the young children in learning a skill for life and by hiring a venue which has a minimal cost I can keep the prices very affordable for families in the area.

#4 *Marketing.*

Easy, target your schools. Most schools have newsletters that you can pay a small fee to advertise that reach a large audience, you can put a notice on your local community board, and to start with you can call your friends and ask them to support you. People will see value in what you are doing if you genuinely show them what you are about. Contact your local paper and run a $14 ad, and your local TV station has community announcements too which usually run for free. You can also do a letterbox drop. It's free and great exercise. Get your friends and your kids to help. Go to the homes that you know your target market live if you know the area well. If not knock on doors and find out who the go to neighbour is. Every street has one...you know the Esme of the street. They'll be your best PR.

My kids asked their friends to see if they would like to learn how to sew. I had a great response by the kids sharing the story at news time. You can always print out invites and ask the school if you can distribute to the classrooms. Some experts call this direct mail marketing.

#5 *Write out the programme.* Yes you have to do this to be successful.

I like writing out the full term and having building blocks whereby the last class is a building block to the next class. You need to set aside block time to write this. Ideally a good chunk of time is the best, but for most of us, that is more of a fantasy than a reality, so just chip away at it one day at a time. Or if you are like a lot of people I know, just work out the next lesson before you get to class.

Document everything. Make templates out of it.

- ☐ *Disclaimer forms*
- ☐ *Schedule of fees*
- ☐ *Permission for audio or video footage*
- ☐ *Program outlines*
- ☐ *Referral forms*
- ☐ *Feedback forms*

Each lesson compile into a work book so you can duplicate term after term, year after year, area to area. That way you are duplicating you too. This then becomes an online workbook for the future so that you can license it or franchise it .

#6 *Once you start teaching, film it. Document it.*

Take before and after pictures. Take footage of people making it. Take as much live footage as possible. Then you can have a sewing on line DVD for people at home to follow.

By filming then and there you are capturing the essense of the class and enthusiasm is infectious.

Besides you are creating stars in the making. You can upload to You Tube and this may also create you own TV show or magazine column.

#7 *In the meantime you're making money.*

It literally can take a week to set up, less time depending on your sense of urgency.

Also promote excitement. At the end of the term, we have puppet shows, fashion parades and mini markets. A great way for the kids to showcase their wears and make money too.

Quick tip: Remember the holiday and the party market too. A great way to make money!

8 *Once you start making money, then set up your website and start selling online.*

Once you're all set up online link it to your Facebook page, divert traffic to your website, capture your leads and then sell your products. Just keep adding massive value.

This is such a fun way to make money fast and it helps and serves more people than just yourself. So I challenge you.

What is your passion and what can you do right now that will convert what you love into money?

There are more tools and templates available on www.mifestyle.com for you to download for free and an outline for your programme.

Simply cut and paste what you need and add what is specific to your business.

Check out www.sewfunky.com.au. to register to become a Sew Funky owner in your area or email info@sewfunky.com.au.

Here's a brainstormer for you to start right now.

- ☐ What am I good at?
- ☐ What do my friends always compliment me on?
- ☐ What do I love doing in my downtime?
- ☐ What do I always dream about doing?
- ☐ If I wasn't doing what I'm doing now for a job, what would I love to do?

- ☐ Who can I help?
- ☐ Who would benefit from learning this?
- ☐ What would the ideal age of my client be?
- ☐ How many people could I teach at one time?
- ☐ How many people will fit in the venue?
- ☐ How may people can I serve without compromising on value?
- ☐ How long will this take me to get together?
- ☐ What is my ideal income for the week, month or term?
- ☐ Is this to supplement my income or to replace my current income?
- ☐ Is this duplicatable?

Come up with your own question.

You are only limited by your own imagination. The tools I have given you are a great start to getting to where you want to go in making money fast. So make a start. Start jotting down ideas right now and then check out the website. There's lots of great ideas, tips and tools to get you going.

So are we there yet? Yep, we sure are.

Good luck.

Learn, create, prosper.

Dee Havebond

Tip #37: Create a Finding Money Club

If you've been doing some of the brainstorming exercises I've suggested, you may be finding it difficult to generate a lot of good money-making ideas all on your own. Remember the old saying: "Two heads are better than one?" Well, it's especially true when it comes to making money and the more heads, the better! To get some fresh perspectives, get together with some of your friends who are creative and supportive and see how much fun you can have coming up with good ideas!

For a bit of excitement, try having a money-making contest. Set a budget and a time limit and see how much money each team can make. It may sound tough, but it can actually be quite easy to pull off. Better yet, the results can be more lucrative than you'd imagine!

When my friend Chad was in university, one of his business professors held a money-making competition. The starting budget was just $5.00 - meaning that was all each team could spend on start-up costs - and they had one week to generate as much money as they could. One team started a tutoring service, another started a proofreading service, and another held a yard sale. The team that made the most money used the $5.00 to buy marshmallows, sugar, and rice cereal to make yummy treats. They sold them on campus until they'd made the money to buy more ingredients, and by the end of the week, they'd netted $3,600! Imagine where that little venture could go! It's one of the thousands of examples of simple ideas turning into big profits.

The great thing about having a group of people together with the common goal of finding more money is that you've also got a team of people who can join forces on any money-making projects - such as the ones above - you choose to undertake. Working with like-minded people can be wonderful because you'll get support, ideas, and motivation that you might not have if you were working all by yourself.

Once your finding money club has developed a reputation for its ability to generate cash, it may be time to start advertising it to the general public. You could sell subscriptions to newsletters filled with your best money-making ideas, charge admission to seminars that you hold or host, or even invite other people to become members of your club for a monthly or yearly fee. It's a fantastic way to put some extra money in your pocket while helping others do the same.

Tip #38: Could You and Your Partner Be Working Better Together?

In a business relationship, it's obvious that you need to communicate about your financial situation. Your business needs to meet its short- and long-term financial obligations in order to prosper and be prepared for the future, so it's critical that you and your business partners are clear about what's going on financially in your relationship.

It may surprise you that the same is true about personal relationships. Talking about money may not seem very romantic, but it can improve the honesty in your relationship, reduce stress levels associated with money, and, yes, actually save you some cash.

Many couples struggle to survive on one income, soldiering on to make ends meet by scrimping and saving because that is the arrangement they have settled into over time and they simply have never considering changing their relationship to an updated model.

The reality of the situation is that today, it can be very difficult to support a couple's or family's lifestyle on only one income. Talk to your partner about this. Perhaps they've always wanted to help out but didn't know how or didn't think you wanted the help. Increase your communication to identify common goals and then delegate responsibilities so that you can move forward together, effectively and efficiently.

Your partner could help out by taking on some of the work involved with getting more cash in the bank. He or she could do some hunting for good investments or focus on ways to reduce expenses. Maybe he or she could pick up an extra shift or try looking for a better paying job. We've also talked about the need for brainstorming to get those creative money-making juices flowing. Your companion is likely one of the best brainstorming partners you'll ever find. You just need to get as many ideas out there as possible and then start searching together for the gems.

Another important thing you and your partner can do about your financial situation is speak with an expert to get educated about your joint financial situation. Little things like having a joint account or understanding tax laws for couples can help you save quite a bit of money. Have a chat with your partner about any financial concerns you have - individually or as a couple - so that you can bring those to the table as well when it's time to speak with an expert. You may be surprised with how many expenses you can trim by taking advantage of your status as a couple.

Always keep money discussions as non-judgmental and pleasant as possible. Remember, the objective is to work together to achieve a positive result for all. Money is a major area of angst in relationships - experts say that it's one of the current leading causes of divorce. Like almost everything else in the world, people often have different attitudes about money based on their individual experiences and upbringing. Keep that in mind as you have these talks; be kind to each other and take the time to understand each other's point of view.

Tip #39: Patents, Copyright, Trademarks, and the Public Domain

There are so many different types of intellectual property. Is there anything that you can call your own? Patents, copyrights, and trademarks can apply to many things: products, a design, a process, etc. Even making little improvements on existing products can pay huge dividends.

Many people used to be frustrated every time they stuck their straw through a flat plastic lid on their soft drink and the liquid spurted out of the top. Someone thought that if only the lid had a raised area where the straw went in, there would be some space under it so that the drink would not be sucked out. That person invented such a lid: a simple plastic lid with a raised area in the center through which the straw fit. He sold them to some fast food outlets and made a fortune.

Have you ever had an idea to improve upon a product? Hint: take note of the little things about the products and services you use every day that irritate you. If you can come up with a great idea to improve the issues you find, you could have a patentable idea on your hands!

The patent that made the most money worldwide is reportedly the process of reading a barcode with a laser. This point of sale device changed the way that retail worked from one corner of the world to the other.

Another potential cash cow are works classified as "public domain." After a time - usually a very long time - original intellectual property rights expire. When this happens, it opens up the possibility for you to repackage those works and sell them for profit. Shakespeare and Beethoven are two examples of extremely accomplished people whose works are now part of the public domain. What could you do with those to earn money? Remember to get creative.

If literature or music aren't your cup of tea, just get online and do a search for "public domain" plus whatever topic you might be interested in. Chances are there's some public domain works out there somewhere that you could leverage to create a new income stream for yourself.

Tip #40: Organize a Street Sale

Get your whole neighborhood together to have a street sale. It takes a bit of planning, but it can be a lot more fun and a lot more profitable than a single garage sale. The bigger the sale, the bigger the crowds of buyers you'll attract. Of course, you'll want to have everyone display their items attractively with easy-to-see price tags, just like an ordinary garage sale. However, to add even more perceived value for your customers, consider incorporating some of the following ideas to make your street sale an even bigger success:

- Hold a bake sale at your street sale. Have each house contribute a few of their yummiest goodies so that shoppers will be tempted by the variety of fresh baked treats available. Cinnamon buns, muffins, and chewy cookies are always fast-selling favorites.
- Sell coffee, hot chocolate, or lemonade, which can be made for only pennies a cup and will greatly enhance both your profits and the whole street sale experience for your buyers. You could also buy no-name brand bottles of water wholesale and sell them for a profit. Even if you only sell each bottle for one dollar, you'll still be making about 65 cents per bottle.

- Sizzle sausages and burgers on the barbecue to sell to shoppers. An added bonus: scientists have discovered that people are more likely to spend money when their sense of smell is deliciously engaged, so not only will they be buying food, they'll be buying your street sale items, too.

If you think big enough, your street sale could turn into a powerful fundraiser for everyone involved. You may even want to consider giving some of the proceeds to charity. If you advertise that some of the money generated will go to a worthy cause, people will be even more inspired to spend their money at your street sale, which increases the profits for everyone. If your event is a great success, consider doing it regularly. The crowds will get even bigger as news of your street sale spreads and you develop a strong reputation.

You should also use the sale as an opportunity to buy or trade for goods that you really need around the house but don't have. Chances are good that one of your neighbors has just what you're looking for at a bargain price. Be careful, however, not to overspend. Remember that the goal is to make as much as money as you can to get out of your financial problems.

Depending on what you're selling, how many people are involved, and how much space you need, you may need permission from your local government. Make sure to inquire with the proper authorities before you get too far into the planning stages of your street sale.

A bit of planning will be required and it might benefit everyone if there are tasks assigned to individuals. There will be advertising that needs to be done, classified ads to run in the papers, signage to be created, tables to be set up, and so on. Overall, however, a street sale should be a lot less work and a lot more fun than holding an individual garage sale because there will be more people pitching in and spending time together throughout the event.

Chapter 4: Little Savings Add Up

This chapter is all about helping you identify those little areas in your life where you could be saving money.

Curbing your day-in-day-out spending habits may not seem like the path to wealth, but let me assure you that transforming the little ways in which you spend your money truly will add up into a big difference.

Most people don't realize just how much those little expenditures add up over time. A dollar here, a few dollars there... if you've ever opened your wallet only to discover the cash you thought you had has mysteriously "disappeared," then you understand the phenomenon of unconscious spending. If you can manage to cut out at least a little of that spending, you'll begin to realize the magic of little savings and how they can transform your life.

Tip #41: Make Your Own Lunches

Did you know that throughout the duration of her 25 years hosting her talk show, Oprah Winfrey brought her lunch to work with her each and every day? Surely this was not a cost-cutting measure, but more of a mental attitude that carried over from her less lush days. Oprah Winfrey, who had personal chefs, a cafeteria in the show's studio, and money enough for champagne and caviar for every single meal every single day, apparently saw the value in the simple act of bringing a lunch to work.

I hope that Oprah's practical habit inspires you to resurrect this age-old cost-saving measure in your own life. It's an idea that may seem overly simplistic, but these days most people overlook what can be a major expense because they feel too busy to plan something as basic as bringing lunch from home. Now, I know you're aware that planning something like making lunches isn't all that complicated, but just to make my point, here's what you have to do:

On your regular weekly trip to the supermarket, buy all the makings for a week's worth of lunches. Remember bread, sandwich meat, cheese, etc. Bottled drinks will be cheaper to buy in quantity at the supermarket than from a vending machine, although keep in mind that water is a cheaper and healthier choice. Sound simple? That's because it is! Isn't it wonderful how easy it is to find extra cash with nothing but a little bit of planning?

Let's do another cost comparison. A sandwich and a drink will cost you at least eight dollars from a retailer, but if you bring yours from home, you would easily be saving 5 dollars a lunch or about 25 dollars a workweek. That's about 1,250 dollars a year and remember that these are very conservative estimates. Often people spend twice that much at a sandwich shop and three, four, or five times that much at a sit-down restaurant. Also, if you have a family, these costs can multiply into really serious amounts of cash going to waste. You could literally be throwing 5,000 dollars to 10,000 dollars a year away simply because your family hasn't been taking the time to make their own lunches. How much money could you be saving by applying this simple idea to your life? What else could you do with those hundreds or even thousands of dollars?

If you get tired of the sandwich routine, bring leftovers to work. The evening before, make enough dinner for lunches the next day or, if you don't want to eat the same food two days in a row, freeze the leftovers and bring them in when you're ready. It's a good way to get a bit more variety in your lunches, it's just as economical, and it may take even less time to put together because you've done most of the work ahead of time.

If you miss the treat of eating someone else's cooking, suggest having a little lunch party at your office. Everyone can bring something special in once a week or once a month and you can all treat yourselves to a feast over the lunch break. It's a fun way to break the monotony of making your own lunches, without spending extra cash.

Remember this idea even if you're not working or if you're out for a meal other than lunch. When you're running errands or out for the day, bring food and a drink with you if you expect to be gone over a mealtime. Doing so will help you avoid stopping impulsively at a fast food restaurant or a pricey sandwich shop.

Tip #42: Buy a Coffee Machine for Home and Office

One of the sneakiest and most common money-suckers is that of the daily coffee or tea. Most everyone has a devotion to some kind of "wake me up" beverage and a lot of companies have been quick to take advantage of this. There are lots of ways to save money in this area; you'll be amazed at how quickly the savings add up.

Are you spending a fortune at the local coffee shop? Many coffee shops are now charging five dollars or more for a coffee beverage of some variety, plus the price of the snacks you buy to go with it. The amount of money people can spend on coffee these days is truly astounding. If you're one of the millions who crave that designer caffeine fix, it's time to lower your standards, just a tiny little bit.

Go to a discount electrical appliance store and get yourself a coffee or espresso machine... or two. They're now available for very reasonable prices and yes, they will make you just as good a cup of coffee as you can buy at the coffee shop. Just read the instructions and follow the cleaning and maintenance guidelines to ensure you're doing everything correctly.

Espresso machines run the gamut in terms of cost, but increasing competition has really driven the prices down. You can buy one nowadays at a very affordable price, but even if you splurge on a more expensive one, it will still be less costly than buying your coffees from a coffee shop.

Let's say the espresso machine you choose costs 250 dollars. Let's also say that before your purchase, you used to buy two fancy coffee shop coffees a day for three dollars each (a conservative estimate!). At the end of only one workweek, you'd have spent 42 dollars on coffee alone.

By nixing that expense from your routine, you'd have the nice espresso machine you bought paid for in only five weeks. Thereafter, you'd be paying only a few cents per cup. Your total savings after purchasing coffee supplies such as beans (and remember that this is a conservative example and doesn't include the snacks you've been buying as well) would be at least 40 dollars a week or a whopping 2,080 dollars a year! Think about all the things you could be doing with that money instead!

Now, imagine how much money you've been spending - and could now be saving - if your coffee habit costs you 10 or 20 dollars a day, and don't forget about how much you're spending buying snacks that you could be bringing from home. Kind of makes you want to buy into a coffee shop franchise, doesn't it? With the money you save avoiding that expense, you just might be able to in no time!

Tip #43: Dress Up Your Coffee for Less

If, for whatever reason, you are not in a position to buy an espresso machine, there remains a lot of creative things to be done to boost a basic cup of coffee. I developed a solution to my pricey love of mochaccinos: I make a half cup of very strong coffee. Then I put a half cup of milk into a jar and microwave it for one minute. When I remove the warmed milk from the microwave, I add in some chocolate powder or syrup. Then I cap the jar and shake it for a few seconds. When it is all mixed together, it tastes like the best mocha that any barista has ever concocted, yet it has cost me a tiny fraction of the price. I get my fix and the added lift of feeling super clever and saving a bit of money, too!

As the versions of espresso machines get more sophisticated, more and more used ones are popping up on sites like Craigslist and other community classified ad sites, as well as at garage sales and thrift stores (just like how the old style of TVs are now piling up as consumers all clamor for flat screens). That means you could get a great machine extremely inexpensively or, if you happen to luck out in Craigslist's free category, for no cost at all.

I'd also like to remind you that this tip applies to just plain old coffee makers. If you aren't an espresso drinker, you can still save money by buying an inexpensive drip coffee machine and a few nice flavored syrups; then you can cut out your daily trip to the coffee shop!

One final tip: beware those new single-cup machines that require special - and pricey - discs or cups to make fancy teas or coffees. Before you buy one of those, do a bit of cost comparison. Because those discs are single-use, the price of actually using those types of machines can really add up. Figure out how much you would use a machine like that and how much the supplies would cost before you splurge on the machine itself.

Tip #44: Save on Your Telephone Bills

For your telephone, make sure to do cost comparisons for both land lines and mobile phones. There truly are a lot of choices, so it's in your best interest to check them all out. Also, if you don't know about VOIP, now is the time to find out about it. VOIP stands for "Voice Over Internet Protocol," which basically means that you can make phone calls over the Internet. Often the quality of these calls is just as good as on a mobile phone, and your long distance calls can, in many cases, be almost free. VOIP is also almost always cheaper than long distance calls from a land line. Take a look online to see what VOIP options are available to you.

Two additional (fantastic) options for phone calls are Skype and Google. Both are free and allow you to make local phone calls over the Internet. For long distance, you may have to pay a small amount, but we're talking just a couple cents per minute. An added bonus is that Skype and Google both have built-in video options, so if your computer has a webcam, you can actually see the people you're talking to, which is especially wonderful if you're connecting with loved ones who are far away from home.

Another word about mobile phones: make sure you've got the monthly package that's right for you. Mobile phone companies are notorious for selling their customers inexpensive packages with very few included monthly minutes. Before you know it, you've used up all of your minutes and are paying exorbitant amounts for even the shortest of phone calls. Of course, it's good to limit your talk time in order to save money, but be reasonable with yourself. If you know you're going to use your mobile phone beyond the limits of your package on a regular basis, change to a slightly more expensive package that better suits your needs. You'll end up saving money in the long run.

Oh, and one more thing about phones: do you really need that land line? If the answer is yes, that's fine. However, many people these days pay to have a land line simply because they're used to having them from before the days of mobile phones. If you've got a mobile phone and a great VOIP service, there's a good chance you don't need that land line at all. It might be just the thing to knock $40 or so off of your monthly expenses.

Tip #45: Get Smart About Your Utilities

If you aren't already, start being utility-conscious. Utilities are indeed a necessary part of life, but as with everything else, there is a cost-saving way to go about it all. Virtually every utility you pay for can either be a waste of money or a smart expense. Take the time to research the choices that are most economical.

For cable, here is a staggering fact: when I was single and living on my own years ago, I made a decision to cut off my cable. I told the people who thought I was crazy that I felt that it was ridiculous for me to pay over 600 dollars a year for cable. They were stunned at this number and asked what kind of extravagant cable package I had. They were shocked to learn that I only had the basic package because they themselves had never done the math. Six hundred dollars a year is only fifty dollars per month, which doesn't seem like much, but when you add it all up, the actual yearly cost of the luxury of cable is sobering (and I only had basic cable - what are you paying if you have a fancier package?).

Now that I have a family, it is more reasonable to pay for cable because there are several people in the house who can take advantage of the wide variety of channels. But for little old me to be able to watch the cooking shows when I felt like it was a bit ridiculous. Today, a lot of television shows can be found online for free, which makes yet another case against cable.

For utilities like television and Internet, I challenge you to be honest with yourself about what you really need and how much money you're able to dedicate to these bills, because the costs can really add up. You may want one of those elaborate television packages with hundreds of channels, but is that something you can really afford when money is tight? Also, some Internet companies offer slower connections for a reduced rate, but the reality is that these "slower connections" are usually perfectly adequate for the average user. I have a friend who uses a package like that and, to be honest, I haven't noticed a difference from the high speed Internet I use at home. For less money, he's doing exactly what most people do on the Internet: check email, watch videos, and download files.

For more fundamental utilities like electricity and gas, do your research to find the most cost-effective providers, and then be smart about how you use them. Turn off lights when you aren't in the room. Use fans instead of air conditioning whenever possible. When you must use your air conditioners, keep windows and doors shut. Don't leave your television or computer on when you aren't using them.

You should also look into how much you can save by going green on electricity and other utilities. Most suppliers now offer rebates for making earth-friendly choices. It's a wonderful way to save money and do your part to help the environment at the same time. Also, if your house isn't insulated, you should definitely correct the situation. Retrofit insulation - also known as blown-in or spray insulation - can be installed after your walls are up simply by drilling small holes into the interior of your walls. An insulated home is not only more environmentally responsible, but can slash your heating bills by 30 percent or more. Investing in insulation might just be one expense that will pay for itself in just a couple of months. Even insulating just your attic can make a huge difference.

Tip #46: Ask for Discounts and You Shall Receive!

Over the course of many frugal years of living as a budding entrepreneur, I learned how to stretch a dollar! Honing your eagle eye and bargain hunting skills is key to this strategy.

When shopping, particularly for larger quantities than normal or big-ticket items, get used to asking for a discount. This is especially effective if you are paying in cash or buying in bulk. In fact, if you want to get really serious about this, organize a buying club or cooperative with your friends or neighbors. That way, you can buy groceries, fruit and vegetables, and various necessities in bulk more often.

You'd be surprised how often you can get 10 percent off or greater by simply asking for a discount. Most store owners understand how valuable it is to have a loyal customer who makes regular purchases at their store. It's in their best interest to treat you well because it means that you'll keep coming back and that you'll be more likely to recommend their store to your friends. Often they will be happy to reward you with a discount in exchange for your loyalty and your positive word-of-mouth advertising.

Another great way to get a discount is to ask for the store model of items. Usually major appliances like refrigerators and stoves that have been out on the floor for customers to look at will be available for much cheaper than the ones that are still in their boxes, even though they've never been used. This is also true for furniture; you can get amazing deals on tables, chairs, sofas, bed frames, mirrors... anything that's been used in a furniture store's showroom. Just make sure that the pieces you want aren't showing too much wear and tear.

If you can sew, even just a little, you can also save money on clothing by finding those pieces with loose buttons or a gap in the hem and pointing them out to the salesperson. Usually, all you need to do is tell them that you're interested in purchasing the item but that you'd like a discount because it is damaged. This is a great way to get fifteen percent off or more because salespeople know that items with even slight imperfections will be nearly impossible to sell. Make sure that the fault is only minor, however, because these purchases will almost always be final sale.

In a similar vein, watch for imperfections in everything you buy. Just a little while ago I bought a new purse with a tiny spot of dye missing on one side. I pointed it out to the salesperson and she gave me 10 percent off without me even having to ask. This trick will work on nearly everything: appliances with virtually imperceptible dents, items whose packaging has been opened... any item that is not completely flawless is likely eligible for a hefty discount if only you ask.

Tip #47: Be Good and Wait for Those Sales

For items like clothing or shoes (that you truly need, of course!), be disciplined enough to wait for the sales. Clothing retailers mark new stock up so much because they know people will want the items badly enough to purchase them right away. Impulse buys are one way that retailers take advantage of shoppers; don't succumb to the temptation! Remember that usually the exact same blouse or pair of shoes you fall in love with will likely be available for 20 percent off or more in only a week's time. In a month, it could be marked down by fifty or sixty percent. The longer you can delay that purchase, the more affordable it will be.

The Internet allows us more opportunities today to find sales and shop for discounts. There are many large chains that will email you notices about upcoming sales and offers if you provide them with your email address. If you'd rather not get on another mailing list, just bookmark your favorite retailers' websites and visit them once every few weeks. From there, it will be easy to plot your shopping for the next while. Also watch for coupon codes when shopping online. It's usually pretty easy to find percent-off coupons or free shipping offers if you just do an Internet search for "<company name> coupon codes."

Another option is to check for factory sales or outlet sales that happen from time to time. These events are usually held in large buildings and allow manufacturers to clear out older stock. Often this stock is still in its original packaging and for some reason hasn't made it out onto a sales floor. You may be trying things on in makeshift change rooms that offer little privacy. Avoid the hassle by wearing tight-fitting clothing over which you can slip whatever you'd like to try on, without finding a change room. Also, due to the crowds, it's wise to keep your wallet on your person rather than lugging a big purse.

Tip #48: Focus on Generic Brands

Not only do large chain stores have cheaper prices than smaller specialty shops, but most also have their own generic- or house-brand products. These products are almost always significantly cheaper, but what you may not know is that they're often made by the exact same manufacturers responsible for the better-known advertised brands. This is because those large chain stores have a great deal of purchasing power, so they choose only to stock those products whose manufacturers are willing to supply a no-name brand as well. Manufacturers are willing to do this - to create an identical item that competes directly with their own - because these "mega-stores" are able to sell astronomical amounts of their products.

The next time you're shopping at one of these stores, conduct your own investigation. Take a look at the contents and volume of a brand-name product versus its generic competitor. Almost every time you'll find they are exactly the same. Cereals, board games, juices, cleaning products, personal care items, medicines, clothing... the list goes on and on and on. They are almost always identical in terms of ingredients, contents, guarantees, etc. The only major differences are the packaging and the price, and sometimes you'll even get more product for less.

Tip #49: Buy in Bulk

Another fantastic money-saving idea is to buy in bulk as much as possible. When you are shopping in supermarkets, always compare the price per unit versus the price of items packaged in bulk. It is almost always cheaper to buy in volume. Choose items that you can store and use over time, such as paper products, toiletries, and cooking oils (especially the fancier ones - these can be super-discounted when bought in bulk). Not only will this technique save you money, but you'll also be delighted with fewer trips to the store (and the less you need to shop, the less temptation there will be to impulse buy!).

A word of caution, however, about buying in bulk: always check that the bulk price really is a good deal, because sometimes it can actually be more expensive to buy in bulk (don't ask me why!). Some shops, such as grocers who offer a bulk section, also have a section where they offer their own brands of the same goods. Over years of observation, I have seen giant bins of a product being loaded into these stores. Some of this product is then packaged, shrink-wrapped and labelled with the store's branding. There have been many times where I have found an item such as quick cooking oats from the bin at x cents per 100 grams. The same quick cooking oats have been packaged by the store and put on the shelf at a proportionately lower price. It may be a small difference, but when every cent counts, every cent counts.

Bring a calculator shopping if you need to. Of course, most items that you find in bulk will be significantly cheaper than buying the same number of units separately. Occasionally, though, you'll find a retailer who will actually make the bulk price more expensive. Make sure you crunch the numbers before you buy.

Tip #50: Get a Chest Freezer

Having a chest freezer at home will offer you a lot of savings and benefits. The average residential refrigerator/freezer combo will really only keep frozen foods good for about six weeks. By contract, a chest freezer can keep frozen foods good for about six months!

Seasonal fruits and vegetables are fresh, healthy, and always well priced simply because the store needs to move the abundant supply quickly before it starts to rot. Bringing these foods home, dividing them into freezer bags and storing them in your chest freezer will keep you well fed for months to come. Nutrition experts agree that frozen fruits and vegetables retain nearly all of their nutritional value, so what do you have to lose? A friend of mine has a berry bush in her yard and she harvests those little gems through the month of August. Her stash of frozen berries sometimes gets her into the next calendar year!

The other advantage to chest freezers is that you can portion out some of your lavish and labor-intensive home cooking and lovingly store it away. This will give you home-cooked meals that are just as convenient as takeout or prepackaged meals from the supermarket, yet far healthier, cheaper, and often more delicious! I can't tell you how many exhausted evenings I have arrived home, desperate for a yummy and nutritious meal only to remember the wide selection that I already have waiting in my chest freezer.

Look for chest freezers on sale or second-hand through your online community classifieds, the newspaper, or local estate and garage sales. If you take the time, you should be able to find an amazing deal on a good quality chest freezer that will help you save loads of money. Also be sure to invest in good quality freezer bags and a good permanent marker so you can store and label everything for easy access when you want it.

Tip #51: Buy Meat on Sale and Save Big

One of the biggest advantages of having a chest freezer is that you can buy meat when it is on sale and safely store it for a long time. The amount of money you can save on meat - without becoming a vegetarian, I mean - is astronomical, as long as you do your homework first.

Once you're at the supermarket, start checking out the expiration dates on all the packaged fresh meat. Next, ask the butcher when they normally reduce the meat prices for quick sale. Once you know this information, you'll know the best time to buy fresh meat at super-discounted prices. This can save you hundreds of dollars over the course of the year, even if you live alone. The bigger your family, the more you'll save and, when you're in a money crisis, even the smallest savings are important.

This tip also applies to fish, chicken, and prepared meats like sausages. If you find other great bargains in your supermarket, such as bread or other goodies, these will also keep extremely well in your chest freezer. You'll be amazed at how much money you can put aside for other things simply by using your chest freezer to save deeply discounted food for a later date.

Before you put your purchases in the chest freezer, separate the meats into meal-sized portions and put them in freezer bags. That way you won't waste any extra meat that you thaw out, don't need, and have to throw away. Good-quality freezer bags will also help keep your frozen goods safe from freezer burn, so they will last longer and taste better when you do get around to them.

Some butchers will also order in a whole side of beef or similar product for you. Buying meat in this way will save you amazing amounts of money, not to mention all the shopping trips you'll avoid. Don't worry; you won't have a whole cow sitting in your chest freezer! Your butcher will cut and package it all up for you so that it's ready to take home for freezing.

Tip #52: The 25% Reduction Exercise

You were worried about this one coming, weren't you? Well, don't panic. We've already touched on some of this, but there is a little more exploration to be done here and it's going to save you even more! When I suggest that you reduce luxury expenses, I am by no means suggesting that you reduce the enjoyment in your life; fun can be had at minimal to no cost!

Okay, this may seem obvious, but you might be surprised once you realize how many unnecessary things you regularly buy that you feel you actually can't do without. Go through your bills over the last year and also think about the leisure things you enjoy doing on a regular basis. Write down an itemized list of these on a sheet of paper (or however many sheets you need!). Ask yourself if you consider each of those things to be a luxury or a necessity.

Another way to approach this is to spend two weeks tracking all your expenses. Don't judge yourself; just take notes. At the end of the two-week period, sit down and examine the expenses with a critical eye. Note which items fall into the luxury category. Be honest with yourself here because in the long run it will greatly benefit you.

Now comes the tricky part: I want you to commit yourself to reducing that list by 25 percent. That means that for every four items on your list, one of them has to go. Don't worry - it's just an exercise to force your brain to start thinking about money differently. You can make the real decisions later, so don't be afraid to be merciless.

If you love your cable TV, your magazine subscriptions, your pizza nights when you just can't be bothered to cook, this will be especially tough for you. However, when you're having significant financial trouble, you've really got to be serious about where you're wasting your money. If you've got high-speed Internet at home but you're having trouble making your mortgage payments, you simply have to prioritize.

Even if you're very careful with your money, you still may discover that you've got some unnecessary expenses you didn't even know about. I have a friend named Jenny who shares a mortgage and a credit card with a brother who is very, very bad with money. As a result she has acquired some debt and some bad credit that has made her life very stressful. Jenny works on cruise ships for about ten months a year in order to pay her debts while incurring very few expenses. I sat down with her to talk about ways to reduce her expenses. Aside from her mortgage, her credit card payments, and her student loans, she also had a $500 monthly car payment. She didn't need that car for ten months of the year, of course, but she'd purchased it before she started working abroad, and her mother used the car occasionally because her own car was a little run down.

When I asked Jenny why she kept the car, she told me it was because she liked the convenience of having the vehicle for the two months she was at home and because it was difficult to orchestrate actually selling a car from abroad. I suggested that she ask her mother to sell the car for her as thanks for allowing her to use it free of charge for all those months. When she did go home again, I told her, she could use the proceeds from the sale to buy a cheap used car or repair her mother's vehicle and use that for the short time she was home. Jenny took my advice; now she's free of a stressful $500 monthly payment - money that can go toward other debts - and she's got a few thousand dollars in the bank for a rainy day.

Jenny's story is the perfect example of why it's a good idea to try the 25 percent exercise. Often it can be hard to see which expenses are luxuries when you're so used to just paying for everything and struggling to earn enough to make ends meet. By requiring yourself to mentally cut out 25 percent of your expenses, you push yourself to get creative about what expenses really are unnecessary.

Tip #53: The "Weigh the Benefit" Exercise

Another great trick is to work out how much a given luxury costs you, and then figure out how much you have to work each week to pay for it. Are you happy making that trade-off? Or, try this technique: compare the luxury you're buying with something you wish you had enough money for, like a family holiday or home entertainment system, and decide which is more important to you.

Whatever trick you use, just make sure that you're diligent about it. Remember that part of the definition of a luxury is that it is something that you absolutely do not need. Once you start to see your various expenses in a new light, you'll realize just how much of your spending is unnecessary and how much you could be saving or putting towards costly debt or other, more important expenses.

More good news: getting rid of luxury spending doesn't mean cutting all the fun, comfort, and spontaneity out of your life. Ask yourself what you can do to replace those lovely luxuries that you are now committing to do away with. Sometimes it is easy to substitute an item or event that is dramatically less costly but offers the same amount of happiness - such as with Jenny and her car (in Tip #52).

For you, this could mean going in to work early to use the company's Internet, throwing a party instead of going to the bar, making a trip to the beach instead of going to the movies, using the library instead of purchasing books, magazines, or newspapers... the possibilities truly are endless once you allow yourself to get creative about how you choose to spend your money. Yes, you will be making sacrifices, but once you start to feel your financial stress disappear, I'm sure you will find it's all been more than worthwhile.

Tip #54: Make Gifts Instead of Buying Them

Finding the right presents to buy for family and friends can be expensive and time consuming. Instead of spending ages in the stores, start a tradition of making something special and personal that comes from your heart. You can go to the library and find craft books for inspiration or check out some of these great ideas:

- Bake something delicious and package it in a paper box or a plastic storage container decorated with some pretty ribbon.
- Take some meaningful photos and give them to your recipients, either framed (these can be bought very inexpensively at craft stores) or on a CD. Get great shots at birthday parties, holidays, family gatherings, or just get outside for lovely pictures of nature. You

could also go through pictures you have already and put together albums of old family photos and maybe even make a family tree to go along with them.

- Sew or embroider some pillowcases, table cloths, cloth napkins, or place mats. Nowadays you can buy all kinds of things to iron on fabric, including decorations and even hemming tape, so you don't even have to know how to use a sewing machine.
- Create some gift certificates with colored markers or on the computer for things like massages, babysitting, dishwashing for a week... any type of service you could do for a friend or loved one as a gift.
- Make your own homemade jam. Freezer jam is extremely easy and inexpensive to make. Best of all, it is always a hit with their recipients - just look up "freezer jam" on the Internet to see for yourself. Add a gingham fabric top, tie it on with ribbon or twine, and add your own little personalized tag.
- Create your own candles. If you have lots of old, leftover candles, you can melt them down to create new ones in any kind of mold you can imagine. Just add a new wick and you're good to go!
- Plan a picnic in the park or other similar event. These days, so many people simply have too much "stuff" and would much prefer the gift of spending time with you over just having one more thing to dust, look after, or store.

Spend a little time thinking about what you could offer or make people as gifts. Focus on what will either be free or extremely inexpensive for you and remember that it's the thought - not the price tag - that counts.

Tip #55: More on Gifts - Saving on the Extras

Greeting cards can be a huge expense, so either buy those at discount stores or start making your own. Making greeting cards is fun because you can personalize them for the recipient and occasion. Buy some colored or patterned paper on sale from a craft or discount store, fold it into a card, and then either write or draw something nice on the front or paste on a meaningful photo. Inside, include your very own message of well wishes.

There are also computer programs you can buy to make and print your own cards, if that's something you'd like to try, or you can go online to dozens of websites that allow you to send e-cards for free via email. These cards come in a variety of sentiments, are often animated, usually include music, and allow you to include a personal message especially for your recipient. To find these websites, just go to your favorite online search engine and type in "free e-cards."

Another card tip is to buy boxed cards. They can be a bargain to begin with, but when a store has to move them to make room for new stock, you can find terrific bargains. Bookstores, gift shops, card stores, dollar stores, and stationers will almost always have boxed sets of cards. They are often blank, which allows you to write your own message to suit the occasion and personalize your sentiments. Many of these boxed sets combine an assortment of cards along a particular theme, which adds variety and means you don't have to keep giving out the same card over and over. I always keep an eye out for sales on boxes of cards to add to my stash at home. For example, you can find extremely cheap Christmas cards at the end of the holiday season. Just pick some up and then stash them till next year. I've never regretted these purchases and am always quite pleased with myself when there is a birthday, special occasion, or sudden event that I'm ready for thanks to my cards!

For wrapping paper, the best way to save money is to be one of those people who collect used gift bags. Gift bags are great because they last forever and they can be used to package practically anything. After a party or a holiday, simply collect the gift bags people aren't planning to take with them and store them for whenever a birthday, housewarming, or other occasion arises. Or, if you prefer wrapping paper to gift bags, buy the paper in the off-seasons wherever possible for humungous discounts.

Tissue paper can be had for a song at most dollar stores and offers the opportunity to wrap gifts in all kinds of bold and colorful ways. As for ribbons and bows, I save the good ones that come to me and use them to adorn gifts that I give.

Tip #56: Keep an Eye Out for Great Gifts

If making gifts isn't for you, try this amazing shopping technique: the year-round gift list.

The year-round gift list is simply a list you carry of the people to whom you ordinarily give gifts. Create a chart that has everyone's names running down the side and the various occasions (birthdays, Christmas, etc.) across the top. Keep it on you so that if you come across a neat gift at an amazing price for someone on your list, you can buy it and store it until you need it. It works equally well if you see something that inspires you but costs too much; write the gift idea down and then comparison shop, check online for deals, and/or wait for the big sales.

My friend Fraser uses this technique for his four nieces and one nephew. With all those kids in the family, Christmases and birthdays can really add up! Luckily for Fraser, finding inexpensive children's gifts is pretty easy and because he gives himself the whole year to find great gifts on sale, he ends up saving a lot of money versus making rushed buys at the last minute when he no longer has the luxury of time.

Why not dedicate a spot in one of your closets for pre-purchased gifts? You could even go beyond your regular gift-giving list and keep a little stash of more generic gifts for thank-yous, housewarmings, baby showers, bridal showers, etc. It's such a wonderfully simple idea that can save you so much time and money. By not being forced to buy things during the expensive holiday seasons or at the last minute, you can pick up gifts at your leisure as you find them and often get them at fantastic prices. All it takes is a little forethought on your part.

Of course, one of the best benefits of this little trick (aside from the savings!), is that when holidays, birthdays, and other occasions roll around, you'll already have the gifts waiting patiently to be wrapped and delivered. Can you imagine how much stress you would alleviate by not having to find that perfect gift with no time to spare? Or how unbelievably blissful you would feel at Christmastime if you no longer had to brave the hoards of people rushing through the shopping malls? Trust me on this one; make yourself a year-round gift list and keep your eyes peeled when you're at the stores. You'll be so happy you did.

Tip #57: Re-Gifting - Yes or No?

While we're on the subject of gift giving, let's talk about the infamous practice of "re-gifting." Some people shy away from it because they don't want to offend, but when you're strapped for cash, re-gifting can be a practical and affordable way to give a gift you would never use yourself.

Of course, if you're going to re-gift, you must follow the cardinal rule: never re-gift if you're going to get caught. If your sister gave you a sweater that's too small, don't try to pawn it off on your mom. If your boss gave you chocolate for Christmas and you're allergic, avoid re-gifting them to a coworker. The moral of the story is to think before you re-gift. As long as you're considerate of the original gift giver's feelings, you should be fine.

If re-gifting makes you uncomfortable, try taking the gifts you won't use in for exchange or refund. Many stores will accept returns without a receipt if you're willing to take store credit instead of cash back. If that doesn't work, perhaps you could sell the item on eBay or elsewhere. And if you're still uncomfortable getting rid of a gift, of course it's okay to keep it. Just check in with yourself to see what will work for you.

Tip #58: Eat at Home or Pack a Picnic

We've already talked about saving money on workweek or school day lunches, but there's money to be saved on the weekends too. Keep in mind that breakfast and coffee for two out on a Saturday morning is going to cost you around 30 dollars, not including the money you spend in fuel getting to and from the restaurant. The same meal at home would be a fraction of the cost, less than three dollars for a huge breakfast of pancakes, eggs, unlimited orange juice, and toast. However, if you just really want to get out of the house, put some hot coffee in a thermos, pack some freshly baked muffins and jam, and go eat breakfast in a park somewhere with the sun shining and the birds chirping.

In fact, picnics are a lovely way to enjoy any meal outdoors with your family or friends. In addition to food and drink, you can bring along games, sports equipment, and music for a pleasant time out together. Get some fresh air and good food out under the stars or on a sandy beach. Even if the weather isn't cooperating, you can move your picnic into your living room. This is a great idea, especially if you have younger kids. Just spread a blanket out, put on some fun music, and lay the food out right there on the floor - your family will have so much fun with the change of scenery even if you're only a few steps from the kitchen.

Keep the "eat at home" concept in mind even for non-mealtime activities that usually include food, like going to the movies. Movie snacks are so expensive; save money by renting a movie or watching one on TV and making the snacks yourself. You'll end up saving about 10 dollars per person on snacks alone, never mind the cost of the movie tickets!

Tip #59: Shop for Savings on Fuel

If you have a car, make a habit of checking out fuel prices daily online. A great website is www.gasbuddy.com, or you can simply search the web for "fuel prices in <your country>" or "gas prices in <your country>" for the best deals in your specific area.

Buy fuel on the days when it is traditionally cheaper; there does seem to be a definite trend for which days are the cheapest. Prices can even fluctuate throughout the course of the day, so check back often. Also, use fuel discount vouchers wherever possible to compound your savings. Keep those vouchers in your glove box so you've always got them handy when you need them. Remember that fuel for your car can be very costly, especially if you drive a lot, so it's worth your while to shop around and use those vouchers to get the best deals available.

Whenever you do find cheap gas prices, be sure to fill up your tank; that way you won't be kicking yourself when your car is back on empty but the prices have skyrocketed!

Tip #60: Driving on a Budget

Before we leave the subject of vehicles, here are another two money-saving tips: one, plan your travel as a circuit so that you don't have to backtrack during the day, which can waste serious amounts of fuel, especially when you're driving in the city. In addition, the more time you waste not driving a circuitous route, the more unnecessary wear and tear you're putting on your vehicle, which will eventually end up costing you in maintenance fees. Plus, the time you waste in your vehicle will not only increase your stress level, but it will also rob you of precious time you could be spending doing more productive things!

Two, drive at the speed limit; faster driving decreases your fuel economy and increases your chances of getting speeding or negligent driving tickets. These tickets are completely unnecessary expenses that can be astronomically costly. They can greatly increase the strain on your wallet, which is exactly what you're trying to avoid. Drive responsibly to reduce the likelihood of getting these terrible tickets or having an expensive accident. Remember, if you lose your license and have to pay for cabs, you'll really feel the pinch in your pocket!

Tip #61: Smart Insurance Shopping

It's a good idea to comparison shop for insurance, not just for your car, but for your home and other insurances, as well. Often insurance brokers will offer you significant discounts if you get all of your insurance as a bundle from one company. It will be less paperwork and easier on your wallet.

Make sure that you have a reliable, highly reputable broker who is experienced in the particular type of insurance that you need. A broker who is not aligned with only one insurance carrier will benefit you more because he or she will be able to compare and contrast the different packages and premiums to find the one that is most suited to your needs. When setting up the insurance, ask your broker what you can do to reduce your premiums. There are certain actions that can sometimes help, but they can vary widely from company to company. Make sure that your broker is knowledgeable and informs you of everything you need to know (even those things you didn't know that you didn't know!).

Tip #62: Discover Your Local Library and Museums

Rather than renting a movie from the video store or purchasing a membership to a video club, gather up the family and head to your neighborhood library. Libraries usually have an excellent selection of all kinds of videos that you can borrow absolutely free of charge. Whether you're looking for a family-friendly favorite, an old-time classic, a fascinating documentary, or an obscure artsy film, the library has something to please everyone.

It's only a small savings each time you go, but assuming a video rental costs between two and five dollars, you could be saving between 104 and 260 dollars a year if you're renting only one movie a week. Even though it's a modest amount of money, think about what else you could be doing with that cash. These figures don't even include the (often substantial) late fees video rental stores charge for forgetting to return your rentals on time, or the snacks you buy on impulse at the checkout.

Of course, we all know that the library is *the* place for books. It bears a reminder, however, because the amount of money we could all spend purchasing books from a bookstore is absolutely astronomical. Most new books these days cost between 15 and 30 dollars each, but even if you buy your books at a used bookstore, you'll still be paying more than borrowing them from your library. Libraries stock all kinds of literature, from fiction paperbacks to academic textbooks to self-help and travel guides, as well as newspapers and many different magazines. If you take the time to really get to know your local library, you may never need to set foot in an expensive bookstore again.

Make a regular family outing of going to the library. Let each member of your family pick out a book or a movie that they'd like to enjoy. If you don't have kids, the library can still be a great place to relish in some quiet time. Libraries also usually host free activities for adults, children, and families; grab a schedule the next time you go to find out when the activities that interest you are going on. Don't forget about the free Internet that many libraries now have, as well. If you're at the library enough, you might be able to scrap your Internet service at home altogether.

Many library systems have gone online so it is worth it, if you find yourself taking advantage of the treasures in the library to ask for instructions on how you can log onto their site, how you can search it, and how you can reserve items that you find. It's a lot less leg work than hoofing it to the building and is likely to inspire a lot of great ideas too.

If you travel a lot and/or are prone to missing library deadlines, consider investing in an e-book reader such as Amazon's Kindle. Many libraries now loan e-books out digitally, so you never even have to set foot in your actual library. You simply go online, peruse the electronic titles for ones that interest you, then download them for free onto your e-book reader. The library will require you to "return" them, but because everything happens online, you can do so from your own computer.

Museums make wonderful outings too, whether you've got a family or not. Introduce your children to different cultures, history, and art, or go alone for a quiet, educational afternoon. Most museums have enough exhibits to suit all tastes, and many even have interactive displays, films, and games to get visitors more involved. It's a fun, interesting, and inexpensive way to spend a day. To save even more, check with your local museums to see if they offer discounts for certain days of the week or month. Many museums will offer perks like free days on the first Tuesday of every month or free entry for children on a certain day. Just don't forget to pack a picnic so you can avoid those expensive snacks while you're there!

Tip #63: Buy and Sell Through eBay or Consignment Stores

eBay and similar online stores and auction websites have become a massive worldwide market for first- and second-hand items. It is extremely common nowadays for people to use the Internet to find nearly every product imaginable at a lower price than they could find in a retail store. This can be a powerful way for you to sell items you don't want anymore because you're advertising to millions of people at the same time; chances are there will be at least one who wants to purchase what you no longer use.

Old but quality articles of clothing are in great demand as vintage apparel. Some of the used clothing that's just sitting around taking up space in your house could be commanding new or better-than-new prices in a consignment store. What clothing items do you have that no longer fit or that you don't like anymore that could be getting you out of your money crisis? What about clothes you bought that still have the price tags on them or dresses you only wore once for a special occasion? Items like evening gowns and good business suits can be worth hundreds of dollars.

To get started on eBay, simply visit www.eBay.com and follow the directions to set up an account. Once that's done, take a few good digital photos of the items you want to sell. Follow the instructions in your "My eBay" to post an ad for your item that includes the photos you took. If you don't have a computer, take your items to the nearest consignment store. They will display your items there for you and split the profits with you once they have sold.

For purchasing items like clothing, these same stores can offer you some amazing deals. Check out the Salvation Army, St. Vincent de Paul, and Lifeline shops; you can often find very inexpensive value and designer clothing that people have donated out of their own cluttered closets. One of my friends regularly finds fantastic designer clothes with the labels still on them; she says the secret is to set your intention before you go by imagining the sort of items you expect to find when you get there. She rarely pays over 10 dollars for a designer dress and now her friends (myself included!) are having similar experiences by following her example.

If you take the time to shop around, just about anything can be found at a fraction of regular retail prices. eBay is great for clothing, shoes, electronic goods, musical instruments, appliances, and more. Do your research beforehand and contact the sellers to get your questions answered and make sure they are trustworthy. eBay has a system that tells you how satisfied a seller's buyers are and how many transactions they've completed - don't buy from someone with lots of unhappy customers. Before browsing or bidding, set a maximum price you are willing to pay for an item, and don't get carried away in the bidding process.

Remember that many sellers won't give refunds or exchanges, so be sure you understand the terms before you bid. Check postage rates before you buy too; some sellers overcharge on postage fees. A reputable seller will ship your items at a reasonable rate and give you a shipping discount on multiple items.

Finally, keep an eye out for wholesale or bulk buys. Many people make a living on eBay by finding great bargains and then reselling those items for a profit. If you're interested in following suit, take a look at eBay's educational literature for tips on being a successful seller or read one of the many books on the subject at your local library.

Tip #64: Free Events in Your Community

Each and every community has a variety of free events. These are put on in order to support, build and grow the community, to bring people together, and to generate goodwill. Often they are done to generate money too! And there is no reason this can't benefit you in two ways.

First, find out where local community events are regularly listed. Perhaps your community has a newsletter or website designed to promote whatever is going on in your area. Perhaps the local community center, grocery store, or coffee shops stay abreast of these events (they are a great place for retailers to advertise, after all). Find a way to get on a mailing list so that the updates come to you regularly.

Second, find out if there is an opportunity for you to sell goods or services there through one of your local events. Find out who is in charge of making these decisions and do a little research about what kinds of goods and/or services they like to choose. Do any of these match up to your skill set? For example, your community might be interested in your:

- ☐ Baking or candy-making
- ☐ Back massages or chair massages
- ☐ Handmade soaps or bath salts
- ☐ Fresh picked herbs or flowers
- ☐ Locally grown produce
- ☐ Shoe shines
- ☐ Live music performance
- ☐ Karaoke machine
- ☐ Hobbies - Could you teach knitting, scrapbooking, birdhouse making...?

If your skill set matches what your community organizers are looking for, you might have just created for yourself a brand new stream of income! With some careful planning, you could become known in your area for your expertise or specialized products - and that will help create income for you year-round.

Chapter 5: Reduce Your Debt

Ugh, debt. It weighs on us, it makes us toss and turn at night, it keeps us from achieving our fondest goals.

Part of your master plan to abundant riches is doing away with your costly, wasteful debt. No, it won't be easy, but it *is* possible and you might just be surprised how quickly you can make genuine and lasting change when it comes to your debt.

If you are burdened by debt, take heart: your debt struggles are coming to an end! In this chapter, I'm going to help you approach your debt in a methodical way so that your debt load will decrease efficiently but manageably.

Prepare to say goodbye to those unwelcome interest payments and that heavy weight on your shoulders. A new day is dawning!

Tip #65: Get Organized and Make a Plan

Struggling with debt can be stressful, frustrating, and depressing. Go easy and be gentle with yourself. Your newfound wealthy thinking will help you to get out of debt faster and easier, so you are already making progress.

As with any other project the first step is *strategy*. You must organize your details and then make a "getting out of debt" plan. Without a plan, you may not be focusing your finances in the most efficient manner.

To reduce current balances quickly, you need to have a clear snapshot of your debt details. This will help you form a plan, and is handy when you get down to taking action or need to reference your info quickly.

On a sheet of paper or a spreadsheet, list all the debt you have, to whom you owe your debt, the amounts of each minimum payment, and what percentage of your monthly income these minimum payments make up. The result will be the minimum needed to keep your bills current.

Then, highlight the items of debt with the highest interest rates and which you've had the longest, then aim to eliminate the highest interest rate first. If it seems like common sense, that's because it is; but seeing it down on paper will still help you understand what's going on and spur you to take action.

Your fight-debt plan in a nutshell:

- ☐ On your debt budget plan, circle the debt with highest rate of interest. That one will be the first to go. Organize your bills and include any new expenses that may be coming up fast (taxes, etc.).
- ☐ Make an action plan that suits you and your situation. Any debt reduction plan must be tailored to your particular situation. This is not a one-size-fits-all plan. Use the notes in this section to guide you.
- ☐ Calculate how much money you can manage each month to help pay down your debt. This amount will have to be above the minimum you need to keep your bills current, so check back with the list you just made to see what you will need.
- ☐ Consider talking to debt collectors. If you can arrange weekly or biweekly payments, you'll reduce your debt more quickly even though your payment amounts will stay the same.
- ☐ Save some money, even when you're in debt. It remains wise to keep three months of expenses in savings. Otherwise use any extra savings possible to pay off that darned debt.
- ☐ Use this time as an opportunity to re-prioritize your spending and take charge of your finances again. Be positive and patient, and stay focused.
- ☐ Cut back on spending! Discipline is needed here: it's time to stop putting anything on credit or borrowing any more money. Definitely do not apply for new credit at this time.

- ☐ Move fast: aim to reduce balances as quickly as possible; paying only the minimum amounts is not going to get you out of debt quickly enough. Paying off more than your minimum required payment will not only get your debt down more quickly, it will also look good on your credit score.

Tip #66: Staying Motivated

To stay focused on your goal to get out of debt, you will need healthy doses of motivation, perseverance, support, and flexibility.

Your motivation will be fueled by lots of big and powerful "whys" - those burning reasons that drive you to get out of debt. What will it mean to you to be debt-free? How will you feel? How will your life be better? Being mindful of how these "whys" fuel your motivation and help you to avoid falling back into the bad habits that started your money troubles. Your "whys" need to be powerful to you personally, so make sure you think long and hard about them and then leverage that power to keep you on the path to financial freedom.

Perseverance is key because getting out of debt will take some time. You didn't get into this problem overnight, so it's unrealistic to expect yourself to get out of it overnight. To stay on track, you will need to find ways to stick with your financial goals even when the going gets tough. I'm positive that you have persevered in something else before; think back on those times and draw on their lessons and the ultimate success you had to help you stay focused.

Of course, your power to persevere will be even stronger if you have adequate support. Getting out of debt is a project like any other and enlisting some support will help you meet your goals sooner. Choose an "accountability partner" if you can and declare a commitment to one another to be motivational and supportive. If your partner is on the same financial quest as you, great. If not, you can motivate and hold your partner accountable in other ways, such as a weight loss goal or a home organization plan. Whatever your particular relationship is, being accountable to someone other than yourself is a fantastic way to help ensure you keep moving in the right direction.

As you develop and execute your plan, allow yourself to be flexible. Review, revisit, and revise your plan as much as necessary as you go along. Your initial plan is your first draft to be used for direction, guidance, and inspiration. If you get off track, simply forgive yourself and move on. Perhaps that means getting back to your original plan or perhaps there are some things that aren't working for you that need to be tweaked. Either way, a little flexibility will help you stay positive about the changes you're making in your life.

Tip #67: Shift Your Loans and Credit Card Debt

Credit card debt is expensive, but there are things you can do now to reduce the amount you're paying, even if you can't pay everything off right away. One smart option is to apply for the lowest interest credit card you can find and then transfer your debt from the higher interest cards to your new, lower interest card. Some cards even offer zero interest on balance transfers, on either a temporary or permanent basis. If you try this, double check that you aren't just getting a low introductory interest rate that will convert into a sky-high rate in a few months' time. Make sure that you read all the fine print before you commit to anything.

If you can't find a credit card with a low enough interest rate, try looking into lines of credit. Many banks offer them; they are similar to credit cards in that you can spend and repay them as much as you like up to a certain credit limit, but they are also like ordinary loans in the sense that you are borrowing money at a much lower interest rate than you would get on traditional credit cards. Opening a line of credit and then transferring your credit card debt over to it could be just the thing you need to dramatically reduce the amount you're paying in interest.

No matter which solution you use, try your very best to pay that debt down as quickly as possible. Credit card interest rates are brutally high and they can make your debt seem completely insurmountable. Always pay as much as you can every month so that the interest doesn't accumulate any more than is absolutely necessary. When extra cash does come in, it's a good idea to put it straight toward your credit cards. Internet banking is great for this because you don't need to wait for your bill to make a payment. All you have to do is log on to make a quick payment to your credit cards whenever you have the spare cash in your bank account.

Lastly, a word of warning: don't get yourself into even more debt trouble by obtaining a new credit card or line of credit and then using it for more overspending, even if it is low-interest. Treat that new credit as a means to bail you out of your old debt only. Make this rule for yourself now: never allow yourself to view new credit as money you can spend and never frivolously use the freed-up credit on your old cards until the old debt is taken care of. If you have to, stop taking your cards to the store. It will be difficult for a while, but you'll be relieved once you discover how much money you're saving in interest fees.

Tip #68: Pay Your Bills on Time!

Another transparently simple but worthwhile tip is to always make your credit card or loan payments on time. If you don't, you risk incurring late fees on top of the interest fees. These will only add to your debt and you may be required to pay interest on the late fees, as well as your regular balance. Even if you can only make the minimum payment, make sure you get it in on time. Making payments on the Internet is a great way to get this done quickly and conveniently, although be aware that many banks require a couple of days before your payment actually gets to your creditor - plan ahead accordingly. Call your bank, credit card company, or visit either of their websites to learn more about paying your credit card bills on the Internet.

If you're having trouble remembering to make your payments on time, use an online personal planner to send you an email reminder. If you have free Google account, for example, you can set up your Google calendar to send you an email whenever you have a task coming up. You can even set up your tasks so that they recur every month at the same time. Just input "Pay bills!" on the day you need to pay your bills and then have Google send you the reminder. You can even put in another task a few days before to remind you that you'll have to be paying your bills soon. (You can find complete instructions for this right in Google's calendar.)

By the way, this tip applies to all of your bills. With just about every bill you can imagine, if you don't pay on time, it will cost you extra. Save yourself the headaches and the wasted money by planning ahead to pay your bills when they need to be paid.

Tip #69: Get to Know Your Credit Card

Creditors can get away with a lot when you don't understand your cardholder agreement. They will use your lack of knowledge to their advantage, so fight back by getting to know what's going on with your credit card. Read the fine print and call the toll-free number on the back of your card if there are any points you don't understand.

For example, when does your interest accrue? Most credit cards charge interest on your balance daily, but don't show you the interest adding up day after day until it's all totaled on your monthly statement. If this is your case, it may be wise to pay a bit extra weekly or biweekly in order to reduce the overall interest total. Try "beating the bank" by dividing the monthly minimum payment of your credit card by four and pay this amount on the same day each and every week. Although you're paying the same amount each month, because you are paying sooner, you are reducing the balance on which interest is charged more quickly. Seen this way, an amount as small as one itty-bitty dollar extra per week will help you pay down your balance more quickly because you'll be accruing less interest over time.

Here's the math for you: if your current monthly minimum payment on your credit card is 200 dollars, divide this figure by four and pay this amount (50 dollars) each week. That feels easier than the full amount all at once and also eliminates any anxiety caused by waiting through the month until taking action on your credit card debt.

When it comes to so-called "interest-free offers," be sure you know what you're actually getting yourself into. For example, you may get an offer in the mail for no charge, interest-free balance transfers when you sign up for a new card, but these offers are often temporary. The creditor is counting on you not paying off your balance in time, so eventually you'll be paying them interest, which of course makes them money. Worse yet, often your new interest rate will be sky high.

Even if the interest-free balance transfer offer is permanent, the creditor still has an incentive to offer it to you: namely, the assumption that, because you have debt, you aren't great with money. In other words, the creditor is aware that you carry a monthly balance on your credit card and is banking on the likelihood that you will incur new debt above and beyond your balance transfer, which will be charged interest.

The moral of the story is that credit card companies are always out to make money off of people's inability to use their credit cards responsibly. If you are well behaved with your cards and can use them without carrying a monthly balance, then they can actually be a great thing. However, if you're like most people and can't seem to pay your cards off in full each month, then you are a credit card company's dream customer and they will take advantage of you as much as possible if only you give them the chance.

One positive thing about getting these credit card offers is that you can take them to your own credit card company and see what they'll do for you. Most people don't realize that their interest rates and card terms are negotiable. Simply call up your creditor, let them know you've been offered a card that is a better deal than the one you have with them, and ask what they can do for you. One ten-minute phone call might be all it takes to get your rate lowered!

Tip #70: Will That Be Cash or Charge?

Do you make purchases on your credit card? How about on your bank card? If so, it's easy to feel a bit distanced from the purchases you make.

Remember the good old days when you had cash in your pocket and when that was spent there was no more spending until you earned more money? Those were the days when living within your means was not only preferable, it was much easier to do because there were far fewer credit card companies around. Granted, there are tough times in life where we need to use that credit card in order to survive or in order to grow; the trick is being able to discern when you've encountered an actual emergency and when you're simply being frivolous with your credit.

If you know for sure that you can charge purchases on your credit card and then pay off your bill in full on time, each and every month, then a credit card becomes a fantastic tool because you are actually borrowing money for the short term interest free. Month after month, your actual money stays in your bank account longer and thus accrues more interest, which is a smart way to spend (and also very annoying to the credit card companies who are counting on irresponsible spenders to stay in business).

Another benefit of many credit cards is the perks they come with. Some cards offer complimentary travel insurance, rental car insurance, priority access to entertainment venues, etc. Many also give points towards travel, a percentage of your purchases as cash back, and more. Again, if you are responsible with your credit cards, this is a great way to earn rewards you can use to purchase things for free down the road. I've used my credit card points for free flights, coffee shop gift cards, movie theater tickets, and Christmas gifts.

Like I've said before, if you are meticulously well behaved with your credit cards, they can actually help you save money and build wealth. However, for most people this is simply not the case, and if you are one of those people, your credit cards are your worst enemy. Do yourself a favor and stick with cash. Simply check with the new budget you made earlier in the book, withdraw that amount of cash for the week, and go from there. If you stay on budget, you shouldn't need any more money than what is in your purse or wallet.

The exercise of switching to an all-cash lifestyle is a simple and very sobering way to keep spending in check. It can also be fun; make it into a game by telling yourself: "I have x dollars to get me through the week - here I go!" Then get creative so you're able to meet the challenge with enthusiasm. Do something productive with any money you have left over at the end of the week; the obvious goal is to put it toward your credit card debt, but if you need a bigger morale booster, try putting it toward your mortgage or depositing it into your emergency fund or vacation fund.

Tip #71: Consolidate Your Debts

Take a personal loan from the bank or redraw on your mortgage to pay down expensive debts such as credit cards or loan shark balances. There are also special debt consolidation loans, which will amalgamate all of your debt into one place, to be paid off with a lower interest rate, so you will get out of debt faster than if you left your debt as it is now.

Choose your lender carefully; compare all of the options available to you and ask as many questions as necessary to determine which lender is right for you. You will find that different loan arrangements have very different repayment requirements and associated costs, so take your time in choosing. Be aware that some lenders penalize you for paying a loan off early, so make sure you check into that before you make any commitments.

Also, if you are choosing to use a debt consolidation firm rather than "DIYing" your loan consolidation, choose one that offers their services for free. Many companies out there claim to drastically chop your monthly payments and fight your creditors on your behalf, but charge such exorbitant fees that you could end up in even more financial trouble. A true, honest debt consolidation company is usually government-run or at least a non-profit organization who will offer you counseling and debt consolidation assistance for free.

The objective is to use lower-interest lending such as home loans, personal loans, or car loans to reduce higher interest loans. The interest rates on high interest loans and credit cards can be crippling when you are having trouble paying off large balances. It may seem stressful to go through the process of debt consolidation, but just think about how much money you'll be saving. Wouldn't it be nice for your monthly payments to help pay down the principle of your loans or credit cards instead of just going toward wasteful interest?

Tip #72: Credit Card Temptation - A Reality Check

If you are like most people I know, you get offers of credit arriving in your mailbox from banks and retailers all the time. Many shops now offer credit and some make it hard to refuse by enticing us with no-interest loans for a period of months or years. This easy credit wasn't available for previous generations, so many of us simply lack the training or skills to know how to manage such temptation.

Look at it this way: on average, people are living twice as long as they once did, so you'll need to save up for a much longer retirement than your ancestors had to. Yes, many of us want new cars every year or so, new furniture, clothes, tools, etc. Unfortunately, the reality is that credit is simply not free money. You will have to pay it back eventually and the longer you wait, the more expensive it gets. The more expensive it is, the less money you'll have as you age to buy the things you need and want. So, do your best now to exercise discretion before using or getting new credit.

If you know that you have trouble with temptation, try this crazy-but-effective trick: freeze your credit cards in blocks of ice in the freezer. It may sound silly, but this is an ingenious little way to stop you from using your cards on impulse purchases or other unnecessary things. Be warned: I am advised that credit cards do not microwave well!

Tip #73: Stay Inspired With a New Approach

It may seem far off right now, but prepare to congratulate yourself like crazy once you've paid off the first of your debts in full. Won't that be wonderful? Then, keep the momentum going and apply your new debt reduction skills to the next creditor. Be patient and persistent. Remember, it took time to get into debt and it will take time to get out of it. Meanwhile, applaud yourself for your diligence, commitment, and integrity at taking this task on. A lot of people simply hide their heads in the sand when it comes to the issue of debt; taking action takes courage!

From a financial perspective, it makes sense to tackle the largest balance first. However, if you're feeling overwhelmed by monthly bills, why not try a different approach and take care of your smallest debt first? It will be less work to pay off than your larger, longer-term debts, which means you'll get more of an "instant gratification" boost, which may be just what you need to keep you inspired enough to deal with the rest of your debt. The best thing you can do for yourself is sustain a long-term trend of better money management, so any steps you take in that direction can only be seen as a good thing.

No matter what you decide, tips for getting out of debt are only going to be useful to you if you take control and make the firm decision to reduce your debts on your own. With patience and determination, you'll be debt-free before you know it.

Tip #74: Expert Insight From Patricia Gibson

Why I'd Like to Say "Count Me Out & Don't Ask Again," by Patricia Gibson

www.tricgibson.com

http://Facebook.com/TricGibsonYourPsychologist

You know which club most of us belong to and wish we didn't? Yes, the Worry About Money Club!

Whether you are in business or it is a personal anxiety, money is one of the most emotive subjects on the planet. Most marriage and relationship breakdowns cite money differences as a significant element in the discord. Ditto in business partnerships - if you can't agree how to run the money then most other things are irrelevant to the business' success.

So, is the answer to have the skills to make everyone else involved in our money matters operate as we would? I would be lying if I said that the thought hadn't crossed my mind, but then at various times throughout my life's journey, so have other impossible and unhelpful ideas.

Money is such an interesting topic, because it is like a microcosm, your world in one subject, and usually represents how we operate on many other levels and on other topics. Therefore, it is important to take an objective look at the foundational ways in which you relate to money. These considerations are relevant for business and personal life.

What meaning does money have for you?

Many people believe this formula:

Money = Self Worth

This equation represents one of the greatest mistakes in thinking and believing. It directly links your financial position to your worth as a human being.

Sometimes in a business or personal partnership, a higher-earning individual may believe that his/her own wishes are more important and should be given preference, due to the fact that they provide a greater financial contribution.

Now, incentives work well: produce more income and receive the benefits (a cool car, vacations, a nice house...). It is not incentives that I'm talking about. It is a personal belief that someone is a better person or more intrinsically worthy due to their income status.

This "crazy" equation causes havoc when a person's income decreases.

How many times has a woman who reduced her income to raise a family battle with the feeling that she doesn't have the same '"rights" in the household as far as decisions about money go. Equally, a man who is financially contributing to the family can feel enormously threatened if he is laid off or takes a lesser wage, as he often feels that he is letting the family down.

For either party this can lead to stress symptoms or even depression.

What/Who influences you about money?

We are currently blasted with fear-based talk about the economy. We put poor-quality messages into our conscious and subconscious when we over-focus on news and messages of limitation.

Now, I can hear some of you thinking, We live in the real world and our financial worries are real! Isn't it important to face reality, especially with money?

Yes, you do live in the real world - and the solution is to stay optimistic enough to allow new thoughts and creative ideas to come to you so that YOU are the creative force behind the real world you want to create.

You can live in your world where you believe that you can make your business/family finances a success and find ways to act on that belief, while acknowledging that some of the outside world is having a different financial experience and different beliefs. You can acknowledge and notice and not let outside circumstances have an impact on your beliefs and actions of success.

It has been proven in Brain Based Leadership Studies that a stressed person has less capacity to remember, organize, and produce (even with tasks that they know how to do) when they are stressed.

So use your brain, literally. Know how to get the best from it. That means look for the opportunity, even within a challenge.This will assist not only your capacity to come up with the new good idea, it will also allow you to process it and organize yourself and your resources so that you can carry out your plan and get a result.

Even in the worst of times, people thrive and some build empires.

The difference is not about the money they have or have lost. The difference between thriving and failing is your beliefs you carry about money.

We have all heard the following beliefs:

- *Money doesn't grow on trees.*
- *You have to work hard to get money.*
- *Nothing is free.*
- *What I enjoy now I'll pay for later.*

These beliefs and many more come under the category of LIMITING beliefs, which are all based on one thing: fear.

It is impossible to have optimism/hope and fear/restriction at the same time.

Which one do you choose?

Does this mean that we ignore responsible behavior? Absolutely not!

Responsible planning with an attitude of enthusiasm will lead you to the next best step in your success. Responsible planning with a fear of failure will surely lead to exactly what you fear.

Keep the responsible planning and do it with JOY and an expectation of success.

Look at your beliefs about money. Take the time and write down the beliefs about money that you know have influenced you/are influencing you now. You probably learned them from parents, business models, and people with whom you mix.

Write down your beliefs about money:

Writing them down is a great strategy because in order to write something down you have to translate it from a feeling into a thought - with actual words - which adds clarity.

Once out of your head and on paper, you can look at it more objectively and then decide whether you carry limiting beliefs or empowering beliefs for achieving your goals.

Your beliefs about money will be directly related to your self-esteem around money, and this links us right up to the first point in this article - the You and Money equation.

Here are some equations with limiting beliefs that I have assisted clients to work with and positively change:

- *Money = Self Worth*
- *Earning less money than my partner = I am not as valuable in the relationship*
- *Earning less money = I do not have as much control*
- *Earning less money = I am not as smart/I do not have enough potential*
- *Earning less money = I am not as free/my choices are limited*

Here are some empowering equations that some of my clients have chosen to take on as their true belief:

- ☐ *Money ≠ My Self Worth*
- ☐ *I am not my money and my money is not me.*
- ☐ *I have the capacity to create new opportunities, no matter what the current situation.*
- ☐ *My real work is to feel abundant, know what it will be like to have the financial goal I desire and then ACT AS IF I were already experiencing the outcome.*
- ☐ *My better feeling and attitude will energize me to complete the action steps required to put my financial plan into place and achieve my goal.*

"Lack of money is no obstacle. Lack of an idea is an obstacle".

- Ken Hakuta

Chapter 6: Ask for Help

Growing your individual wealth is not an individual process.

Of course, you will need to hold yourself responsible for your end of your endeavors, but enlisting the help of others will help you earn bigger personal and financial rewards far more quickly than going it alone.

Asking for help is not a sign of weakness - far from it. The ability to recognize and ask for the help that you need is the single best way to help ensure your path to riches is as unencumbered as possible.

Enjoy the process of involving others. You'll enjoy the company, you'll get the support you need, and you'll feel far more motivated than if you were working all by yourself. Besides, what good is unimaginable wealth if you don't have your friends and family to share it with?

Tip #75: Ask for Donations

Another strategy for finding money is simply to ask for it. This can be very uncomfortable for most people, but it really does work. Churches, volunteer groups, and charity organizations have been using this technique for generations because they all know that people are willing to donate to causes that they feel are worthwhile.

A respected friend of mine knew that she could turn her whole life around if she could just attend a certain personal improvement seminar. Unfortunately, she didn't have enough money to pay for the attendance fee. Being an unemployed, single, full-time mom, my friend knew that the only way she'd get to that seminar would be to swallow her pride and ask people for the money. She started door-knocking and in a very short period of time, she had raised half of the money she needed simply by telling people her story and asking for a dollar from each of them to support her cause. Most people gave her much more than a dollar each, and another friend was so moved by her story that she gave her the balance of the attendance fee!

If you feel too embarrassed to ask for the financial help of others, take a moment to think about how much better a given situation could be for you if only you had the money to take care of it. Of course, it isn't something you want to overuse with your friends and neighbors; you don't want anyone to feel that you are taking advantage of their generosity. However, if you feel that your cause is worthwhile, chances are your friends will, too. You may be surprised to discover that most people are delighted to help a friend in need, if only they ask.

If you truly can't overcome your pride in this matter, perhaps you can ask people to loan - rather than donate - the money to you. Since you are only asking for small amounts of money from many people, you'll find that virtually no one has a problem lending to you and waiting until you've got a steadier cash flow to pay them back. When you do pay them back, chances are these people will be happy to have helped you out and more than willing to invest in you again and again.

However you decide to collect your donations (as gifts or loans), make sure that you tell each and every donor what their contribution did for you and what their money helped you to accomplish. It's very important that you be grateful for the gifts that you receive, especially those from your friends and neighbors, so that they can rest assured that their money has not been wasted. It's a simple way for you to give back to those who supported you during your difficult time.

Tip #76: Get the Raise You Deserve

People are often very intimidated by the prospect of asking for a raise, but if you do some research into how much your job pays on average, you may discover that you, like millions of other working adults, are actually underpaid. Remember, there is no reason to be afraid to ask for a raise if you are a good worker. All you need is the confidence to ask the question in a way that your employer is open to hearing.

Put together a well-researched, thoughtful package that outlines how long you've been with the company, what you've achieved in your time there, and how much less you are being paid relative to others in the industry. A quick Internet search will give you an idea how much similar positions are paying currently. If you don't have concrete figures to back up your contributions to the company, try thinking more abstractly. Are you super efficient? Are you a good motivator? Do you help keep morale up in the office? All of these are rare and worthwhile qualities in an employee.

In essence, you are explaining to your employer your value to the organization. You don't need to be pushy or upset; you simply need to state why you deserve a raise. If you present your argument persuasively, your employer will likely find your request more than reasonable, especially if your current pay is not consistent with average market rates. At the very least, it would be way more expensive for your employer to replace you than it would be to give you the raise, so there really is no harm in asking.

Tip #77: Think Outside the Box to Earn More

If you discover that you are already fairly paid, you can still ask for a raise, but you might also want to consider asking for a profit sharing arrangement instead. In this case, you would get a percentage of extra profits from business that you bring in the door. This can be a great way for you to make more money and for you to derive a lot more satisfaction from your job. You'll find that the more directly you can influence your pay, the more passion you'll have at work. If you don't know how to go about this type of proposal, simply ask your employer how you can help them and the business be more productive. This will tell your employer both that you're looking to make more money and that you are serious about contributing to the business, which he or she will certainly respect.

If you own your own business, could you give yourself a little raise by putting your prices up by 10 percent? Most small businesses and service providers are afraid to raise their prices, but if you are giving your customers great service and value, a minimal difference on the price tag is unlikely to turn them off. A difference as small as 10 percent will usually go relatively unnoticed, even if you do this on a fairly regular basis. Keep in mind that you are better off having fewer good, loyal customers who appreciate your work than too many to look after to the best of your ability.

Tip #78: Find Investors for Business Funding

If the money you need is actually capital funding for a business idea or project, trust me when I say that there are plenty of people out there looking for projects to invest in and those people aren't that hard to find. All you really have to do is ask around; ask your friends, your family, your accountant, and your finance broker. Call each one and ask if they know of anyone who would be willing to invest in a business project. Not everyone will be able to help you out, but some certainly will. It just takes a little determination on your part to make those phone calls.

To get the best results from your efforts, you'll need a well written, solid business plan to reference when talking about your idea. Outline your plan of action and explain what return investors will receive on any money loaned or invested. Your business plan is a critical part of the process of receiving business funding, so dedicate as much time as is necessary to get it right. Look online for articles about writing a good business plan or, better yet, set up a meeting with the business department of a university. Many business schools require entrepreneurship students to take a class on effective business plan writing, which usually includes writing an actual business plan for an actual business. Often, you can get a fantastic, comprehensive, and professional business plan written this way, with nothing but a small donation to the university. If none of the schools you approach have a program like this, try emailing professors directly - some might be willing to allow their classes to take on your project.

It is imperative that if you are taking other people's money as seed or investment capital, you must make paying them back in a timely manner your top priority. Your reputation as a trustworthy person and business associate depends on your reliability in this matter. No one wants to lend money to someone who doesn't follow through with a solid plan for paying it back. Remember that integrity in all of your business dealings will only lead to a more profitable organization, as well as a long list of willing people you can turn to in your hour of need.

Tip #79: Get Sponsored for Doing Something Extraordinary

Do you have a personal goal that you have always dreamed of achieving? Do you need attention and deadlines to spur you to action? Does the idea of doing something extraordinary appeal to you?

People have raised huge amounts of cash by getting sponsored to do a variety of things like play golf for days straight, fast for a period of time, or walk backwards from one city to another. Anything that is even slightly quirky is likely to generate enough public interest to garner some serious cash flow.

At weddings, they'll often hold a special raffle. It works like this: guests at the wedding purchase raffle tickets throughout the reception. Near the end of the evening, a raffle ticket is pulled. The winner takes home half of the proceeds from the raffle, with the remaining half going to the bride and groom. Guests are motivated to buy these raffle tickets both because they might win something and because they know that no matter what, part of their money is going to support the newlyweds.

There was a youth minister once at a church I'm familiar with who had a reputation for being... well, hairy. He had one of those huge scraggly beards, a giant bushy mustache, and a dark head of hair so thick and curly that it nearly covered his eyes completely. One day, he announced that at the church's Halloween dance, he was going to shave his head and his beard completely. Now, the proceeds from the ticket sales of this dance were partly to fund the church's youth program and partly to support a local cancer organization, and in the past it had been very sparsely attended. This time, however, church members rushed to buy tickets and turned up in droves, just because they were curious to see what their youth minister would look like with a totally naked head.

Whether people are buying raffle tickets at weddings or turning up in support of a head-shaving event for cancer, the money-generating principle is the same: people will give you money if they know it will be in support of a meaningful cause. Golf-a-thons are often in support of sports programs for underprivileged children. Monies raised from a weekend of fasting go towards aid organizations in underdeveloped countries where people are starving. As long as you take a portion of your proceeds and donate it to a worthy charity, people will support you.

If you hit on a really popular idea, consider building it into a regular event that people can get excited about, look forward to, and attend regularly. You may even want to include more people (imagine ten hairy men shaving their heads instead of just one!) and encourage them to raise sponsorship dollars, as well. If you have a business, this type of event is also a great way to generate public interest in your company and enhance your reputation in the community. You'll be making money not just for yourself, but also for your business and, of course, for whatever worthy causes you choose to support.

Tip #80: Financial and Investment Advisors

Finding the best financial and investment advice is a fantastic way to help grow your money and get out of debt more quickly. However, don't entrust your financial security to just anyone; the advisors you choose must be good at what they do and qualified to provide you with the expert advice you need.

When you meet with prospective advisors, treat the meeting like an interview. Ask questions about their qualifications and experience. See how you feel about them and whether you could see yourself working with them over the long term. Just like when an employer is seeking a new recruit, be sure to interview several candidates before narrowing it down to one. The right advisor for you will respect the fact that you are doing your due diligence and answer your questions accordingly.

When meeting with your advisor, don't be manipulated by the amount of time they spend with you as they discuss your options in terms of financial and investment products. You are not obligated to buy anything presented to you, so before you make a commitment, find out your advisor's intentions regarding the opportunities in question.

Start by determining whether your advisor is tied or independent. A tied agent is affiliated with one particular company and can only sell its products. He or she is legally required to only sell you the products you request but is not required to tell you if another company has a better suited product. Tied agents may be good at what they do, but they are likely to be biased so you will need to take care before you make any firm commitments.

Independent agents sell the products and services of several companies, so they are likely to be less biased toward one particular company or product. However, nearly all of them work on a commission basis, so they may have an interest in guiding you toward the companies and products who offer them the best returns. Again, this doesn't mean the agent is bad or untrustworthy; it simply means the onus is on you to make the best decisions for yourself and your situation.

Again, your best strategy here is asking the right questions. Find out how your prospective advisors earn their money. Do they earn commissions on each sale or are they paid flat fees? Will they stay in touch with you and keep you abreast of new products and industry trends or will they disappear once their commission has cleared? Will they assist you with other financial needs like insurance coverage, tax planning, estate planning, etc.? It's best to have someone skilled help you create a full and comprehensive plan.

As for investments, remember that no financial planner will be able to tell you with certainty which stocks you should invest in or when you should buy and sell. The market is highly unpredictable, especially in these volatile and uncertain times. Any financial advice is best taken with a large grain of salt because not all financial advice will be good; maintain your common sense and think through the advice you get. Too many "professional" planners care more about selling you a particular product than giving you solid information so that you can decide for yourself.

To start your search for a reliable advisor, begin at your local bank or credit union. They may offer these types of services for free or, if they don't, they might be able to point you in the direction of someone who does, especially if you express your financial difficulties. If you can't find a free service, try to locate an advisor who works on a sliding scale so that his or her compensation is commensurate with your own profits.

I really can't overstate the importance of doing your due diligence before you engage someone to help you with your finances or investments. Unfortunately, there are dishonest people out there who will take advantage of you if you let them. Do your homework, get references and, above all, trust your instincts.

Chapter 7: Value-Adding Opportunities

When it comes to finding more money in your life, it pays to take advantage of every opportunity that comes your way.

Of course, not everyone perceives opportunities in the same way. The key is being able to recognize a potential money-making opportunity when you see it and then acting on it quickly, before the chance passes you by.

Start by looking at what you already have, in terms of your possessions, your current job, and your ideas. Where are those money-making ideas hiding? Sometimes it's not a matter of finding a brand new source of income, but tweaking the sources that you already have to function more efficiently.

Let's take a look:

Tip #81: Borrow Against the Equity in Your Property

Many people do not realize that there are circumstances in which lenders will allow the owner of a property to borrow against the extra value in that property. This extra value is somewhere between what is currently owing on the property and its fair market price. Often this difference can amount to quite a lot of money, especially if the property value has gone up after a renovation or an overall increase in the market.

Before we go any further with this idea, let's be clear: I don't recommend that you borrow out of your equity unless you plan to use it to keep your assets as free of bad debt as possible over the long term or unless it is to use the money for another good quality investment. For many people, property is the most valuable asset they will ever have in their lifetime, so borrowing against its value should be carefully considered as part of a long-term plan only. In other words, you should always have a plan to pay that money back. Keep in mind that the penalty for not being able to pay back that loan could be losing your house to the bank.

That said, this strategy might be a solution if you have an urgent need for cash flow or if you intend to use the borrowings for an investment purpose that is likely to earn a higher rate of return than the cost of borrowing the money in the first place. For example, you might use the money from your equity to invest in a good business that will offer - or, preferably, guarantee - a rate of return and/or ongoing income that is greater than the cost of the interest and borrowing fees of the loan.

If this solution appeals to you, be sure to talk to a few lenders to compare their terms and fees. Get advice from a reputable financial advisor or broker. Remember this general rule of thumb: "The higher the return, the higher the risk." Understand the true value of your home and be extremely careful with how you spend it. Finally, be aware that there may be tax implications for borrowing against your property. In some cases, the purpose of the loan will affect the tax deductibility of the associated costs, so check with an accountant before you make any final decisions.

Tip #82: Rent Out Your House

If you are really having trouble making ends meet, get advice from your accountant about where you could be living that would be easier on your wallet. You may find that moving to a smaller home or apartment in a less expensive neighborhood could save you a great deal of money every month. It may also be worth thinking about moving to a completely different city; some cities are much more expensive than others, so if it's possible for you, remember that moving somewhere with lower housing prices also usually means a lower overall cost of living, which means additional savings on virtually every expense you have.

Once you've moved out of your house, you can lease it to someone else at a higher rate than you are currently paying on your mortgage or monthly rent (just get permission from your landlord if you have one). This can mean significant financial savings, which can greatly ease your monthly burdens. If you're an owner, this is an especially great option to consider because it turns your home into an investment property, which means that in some jurisdictions, mortgage and maintenance costs on that home become tax-deductible.

If you've got some extra space in your home, you can also take advantage of this type of idea without moving. Consider renting out your guest bedroom to business travelers or other people in need of room and board. There are all kinds of people out there in need of accommodation of this type because it's less expensive and more comfortable than a hotel, and it's also probably completely furnished. You could even offer your tenants a package that included groceries, home cooking, and cleaning for an additional fee, or discounts for extended stays.

You could also put this idea to use if you've got a basement or a whole floor in your home that you could rent out to a couple or a family. The rent your tenants pay you could cover most or even all of your monthly rent or mortgage payment. If you don't have enough space right off the bat, think about how you could rearrange your home to live in a smaller area so that you could invite others to move in. It may seem inconvenient, but remember that the amount of money you'd save this way could make a real difference in your financial situation. If cash is really tight, this might just be the solution you've been waiting for.

A few additional words of advice: make sure the people moving into your home are trustworthy. A good way to help ensure your safety is to ask your family and friends if they know anyone who is looking for a place to live. That way, you'll be able to speak to people you trust about your potential tenants before allowing them into your home. Also, remember that there are legal and tax implications associated with renting your home. It's important that you seek advice specific to your situation from an accountant and a lawyer before letting anyone to move in, and don't forget to double-check that advice with your local tax office.

Tip #83: Become a Home Away From Home

There are a variety of companies that find room and board for international students in a type of "home stay" program. These companies are a mere Google search away! Although the specifics vary from company to company, the deal is usually along these lines: the landlord offers a room in a family home. The room needs to be furnished with the basics: a bed, a dresser, a closet, and a desk for a person to work at. Meals are usually included too, although you certainly do not have to make everything from scratch. Providing basic fixings is usually acceptable at least for breakfast and lunch. You are at an advantage too if your location is close to or on a direct transit route to a major college or university. In exchange, you will be paid a monthly stipend.

Of course, the home stay program is not for everyone. It is really geared toward providing the international student a comfortable family home where they can be safe and provided for. Many programs will expect you to be the student's "host family," which means you treat the student as a member of your family and help them acclimatize to your customs and lifestyle by including them in family activities and even taking them on family vacations with you. The payments for these programs vary, so check with the company first and crunch the numbers to see if it will be worth your time and effort. If you do look into this option, make sure that you get clear details on all that is required of you in exchange for the monthly payment you will receive.

Tip #84: Take Advantage of Depreciation Schedules

If you have an investment property, particularly one that was built in the last 20 years, hiring a firm to make up a depreciation schedule could bring in some significant savings. If you don't have a depreciation schedule, you could be missing out on about 4,000 to 11,000 dollars minimum per year in tax-deductible savings, depending on your jurisdiction.

If you are serious about being a property investor, I would also recommend hiring an established and independent property analyst to review your current holdings and give you advice before you take on any additional properties. Property is almost always a very strong long-term investment, but it's important to get the right mix of properties. A professional advisor can help you spend your money wisely on properties that have capital growth potential and are neutral or positively geared.

Keep in mind that real estate agents - unless they are buyers' agents - tend to have a bias toward the sellers of properties because it is the sellers who have hired them. Unfortunately, some will tell you whatever they think you'll believe in order to secure a sale. Always do research on your own on any property that you are interested in, including looking into the state of the neighborhood. Never commit to anything without having certified inspectors look at the foundation as well as the plumbing, wiring, roof, etc.

There are all kinds of websites to advise you about depreciation schedules and property investment. Take some time to educate yourself and speak with a variety of experts before you make any serious decisions or financial commitments. Remember that these can be great tools both for making and saving money, as long as you use them wisely.

Tip #85: Renovate and Revalue

If you own property, consider doing a budget renovation and getting your property revalued. Talk to your bank about what they would be willing to lend for such a project and consider hiring a professional, experienced valuer to give you an idea of what extra value, if any, could be realized in the current market. A good valuer will also be able to give you advice on which renovations would be worth your time and money and which would just be a waste.

Good news if you're really strapped for cash: some areas offer rebates for eco-friendly updates. For example, if you insulate your home, swap out your old windows for energy-efficient vinyl windows, or install a tankless water heater, you may be eligible for a hefty rebate or tax credit... which means your renovation might cost even less than you'd hoped.

More good news: your renovation project does not have to be overwhelming, you probably don't have to hire professionals or have any special skills, and in many cases you do not need any outside funding whatsoever. All you really need is the desire to work hard and do the job to the best of your ability.

Perhaps your shabby carpet or linoleum has nice hardwood underneath. Perhaps your dingy walls need a fresh coat of paint. Even things like trimming your hedges and cleaning up your gardens can greatly enhance your house's curb appeal, thus increasing overall value. Simple renovations like these can add a great deal of value to your home. If you aren't sure how to do a terrific job, browse the Internet for tips and tricks about doing whichever specific projects you've chosen to undertake, or ask an experienced friend to help you. Again, just make sure that any renovations you do create value for you over and above what the renovations cost you in the first place.

Once you have added this value to your home, you can sell it for a greater profit, rent it out at a higher rate, or borrow against the new equity you have just created for instant cash flow. Renovations - even simple, inexpensive ones - can really help you overcome some of your existing financial difficulty.

Tip #86: Make Money With Investments

Unless you have some experience knowing how to do your due diligence and evaluate investments, or have a trusted advisor who can give you common-sense guidance that you clearly understand, be wary of opportunities presented as "investments." After losing much of my hard-earned fortune through investments in other people's businesses, I have learned that about 49 out of 50 "great deals" pitched to me don't stack up so well when you know the full picture.

Investing is generally about funding or sharing risk and by that reasoning, the more risk you can afford to take the higher the potential return should be in exchange. So, if you will be wiped out financially by losing part of or all of your investment, then you should carefully consider taking on that risk. However, if the investment represents, for example, a fraction of your cash reserves, this puts you in a safer position to assume the risk and the more risk, the more you should expect the return to be.

It is surprising to me how few people understand this risk-to-reward relationship when they want others to invest in their own product, service, or business deal. Risk tolerances vary from person to person, so an investment that seems too risky for one may seem challenging and exciting or even an irresistible bargain to another. Watching the interest in my bank account grow at a painfully slow rate was not of much interest to me (pun intended!), so I learned quickly that I have a higher tolerance for risk than someone who would prefer to leave all of their money in the bank. However, when I trade or invest in the stock market, I am only using my cache of money that has been earmarked for investing, not the money that is designated for living expenses. So, in that sense, my risk tolerance is lower than someone who would be willing to pour their life savings into the market.

Volatility is a key consideration. For example, you may be comfortable assuming the risk that a day-trader faces. Great... but can you handle the volatility? Will it be comfortable for you to watch stock prices potentially going up and down like a roller coaster each day, or maddeningly staying the same price when you thought they were going to move quickly? Knowing your risk tolerance and overall personality will indicate what level of risk and volatility you can handle in the world of investing. Again, it is possible to make money in this arena, and many do, but be sure to get expert advice before you start. If you're new to the stock market, consider investing in a reputable training course to learn and understand the tools and strategies that are readily available to the educated investor.

Tip #87: Be the Organizer

Many of the wealthiest people on the planet got there through building businesses. Sometimes, the key to making money is simply developing a new business idea in the short term as opposed to running its operations day in and day out for the long term.

Building a business is all about organization. Organizational skills do not come naturally to everyone, so if you have a keen eye for planning and detail, you may have a potential new and profitable business just waiting to be unearthed. Remember, people will pay others to do something they cannot do or do not want to do. Do you have what it takes to get a business that fills a need for others off the ground?

Consider something as simple as a tailor or dress-making business. What needs to happen in order to get started? Your list of required tasks might involve:

- Finding and financing retail space
- Physically setting up shop
- Purchasing and installing the necessary equipment
- Choosing and purchasing fabrics
- Marketing and advertising
- Signing up for and paying all necessary utilities
- Dealing with clients
- Processing orders
- Fitting, sewing, alterations, pressing, and packaging

- Billing and accounting
- (And much more!)

Who on earth would do all this work? Who has what it takes to see the business launch through? The answer is a person who has a strong talent for organization. It isn't necessary that this person know how to sew; he or she must only have the knack for seeing what needs to be done and sorting out how to do it.

If I'm describing you, please know that you have a very rare and valuable talent. Organization can lead to profit if you are willing to coordinate what others either can't or won't. For example, let's take a look at the career of a friend of mine, who is an independent filmmaker. She will have a vision for a project, source it, obtain the rights to it, develop the script, workshop then polish the script, hire a team of producers, hire an entire crew, scout locations, book locations, gather all the necessary funding, get all the permits and waivers, get any documentation and permissions necessary, put out a call for actors, cast the actors, rehearse, source the film equipment needed, physically set up the shoots, book transportation, book the catering and clean up for the shoots... are you getting the picture? She's a busy girl. The entire process from start to finish takes several years and my friend just happens to be one of those gifted, organized people who can take on a task and then see it through to the end, even if the end isn't for a very long time.

Does she do it all herself? No, of course not. Her talent lies in her vision, perseverance, and organizational skills.

If you possess that talent, don't underestimate it and start marketing yourself right away. Have faith in your abilities; for every one of you there are hundreds - if not thousands - who only wish they had the same skill set!

Tip #88: Expert Insight From Denise Hall

How to Build a Mother of a Business, by Denise Hall (aka "the entrepreneurial mother®")

Because I am one, I know that mothers are often also the primary (and even the sole) breadwinner in the family, and both are really BIG jobs! So I share with you seven of the best tactics I use as the entrepreneurial mother™ that have enabled me to build my seven-figure Mother of a Business while not compromising on the important things, especially when on a tight time-budget!

A disclaimer if I may: If my use of the word "mother" does not apply to you specifically, feel free to replace it with parent, father, aunt, uncle, grandma, pop, whatever works really; the principles still apply.

OK, so why build a Mother of a Business in the first place? My intention is clear. Combine role-model mothering and earn enough (plus plenty more) to support our lifestyle for now (and in my old age!), all in guilt-free school hours, and on my terms.

Whilst I figured out the "how" as I went along, the key is that I connect as many dots as possible to use minimum time to earn maximum money. After all, there's no point without travel, fun and comfort in spades as well, right?

Fortunately, as Daughter has grown, so has my Mother of a Business (www.acetalentnet.com.au), to the point where it now ticks along very nicely. Could it grow further? Absolutely. But... I am very wary about doing so as it would impact on our lifestyle of choice. Doable? Yes. Preferred? Questionable!

Optimism and self-belief are definitely a good start but let's face it, it is only a start. You need tactics to give your plan bones, and you need to take action to put flesh on those bones.

It's not about finding oneself; it's about creating oneself!

Without further ado, here are my favorite seven tips (or as I affectionately call them, "mother's little helpers!") for building a Mother of a Business:

- *Find four hours or less a day. Do you even know what your typical day really looks like? Grab a piece of paper and draw a grid with Monday to Friday along the top and school hours in 30 minute chunks down the left-hand side. Now, add in all the usual daily activities you are currently locked into, under the day, next to the time slot. Do you see much white space left? If not, then what can you move or get rid of to create that four hours at most a day?*

- *Earn what you must in four hours or less. This really does take the pressure off and anything else earned outside of that figure is adventure money (well, it is for me!). Knowing what you must earn provides very specific focus and very measurable insight. To roughly calculate what that number is, here's what you do: Using your grid in #1 as a guide, how many hours do you have per year to build your business? (e.g.: grid shows 25 hours per week x 40 school weeks per year = 1000 business building hours). Divide that number into what you earned last year (e.g.: $50,000 per year / 1000 = $50 per hour).*

- *Outsource what can't fit into four hours. I love the word "outsource." Yes it does sound big business, but that's no reason why we can't adopt the same principles to suit us. Okay, tell the truth! What are you doing that gets in the way? What are you not doing that you must? What can be done elsewhere? What don't you want to do and who could do it instead? Make rules. Work out what you want to keep, and what you want to find an alternative for. Then start making inquiries. You'll probably know people that are doing or have done what you're looking for, so talk to them and get it sorted.*

- *DO one thing every day, FIRST THING, immediately after the school run each and every morning. Do whatever is the next thing in your diary or daily to-do list (or whatever you use) first. That way, if life does take over for the rest of the working/school days, it doesn't matter. You've done what you need to do. Think about it; by adding all the ticked-off daily to-dos at the end of the month, you will have done approximately 20 more things towards building that Mother of a Business... It adds up!*

- *Turn OFF the automatic send/receive on your email. Yes, this is classic Tim Ferris (The 4-Hour Work Week) and it so works! Rather than be distracted by emails randomly landing in your inbox with their customary "hello, pay attention" ding potentially taking you completely off track, don't do it. Just turn that function off. You will be pleasantly surprised how much more controlled you feel by doing so. Decide which hours of the week to set aside to handle emails and correspondence generally, lock it in the diary; and that's when you do it, and only then.*

- *Connect the dots. Business is creative. I'm not just talking about what you produce, more about the way you do it. You can structure your Mother of a Business any way you want. Here's an example: at aCE talentNET, we made a conscious decision not to spend money advertising, but we did want to keep putting our name out there, so how to do that? Reciprocal Marketing is a term I coined, and it goes like this. Because we have a large and specific talent pool, others want to get in front of them. If their product/service is selected to be included free in our monthly eNewsletter, we in turn agree to how we are marketed with that same product/service wherever else they're doing so. What can you do that is savvy and high impact, low effort, and low cost?*

- *Start with the end in mind. The best, easiest, and fastest way I know to get a grip quickly on what to spend time on (or not) in your Mother of a Business is to realign it so it can be sold on the spot (if you choose to, that is!). By getting a handle on the most valued elements and renovating accordingly, you highlight the exact places to hone your efforts for maximum payback. After all, what's the point of going through all this effort if you end up packing your Mother of a Business away with the toys once you're done?*

Making changes can be scary, so fake it till you make it! Seriously though, bottom line, if your business or job is eating up your time, and you're way too busy to earn more and mother more, then it's time to STOP. Reexamine, reevaluate, and reenergize. What do you want? Why are you doing what you do? If you're not happy with the answers, it's time to DO differently.

Tip #89: Think Your Way Rich - Intellectual Property

Intellectual property can be the cornerstone to skyrocketing your wealth. I've touched on this in various sections throughout this book. The key element in intellectual property is about leveraging it so that you get paid not just the once for the labor involved, but over and over again. Often, the intellectual property you've created, such as a book, will generate passive income over time, which means that not only is your work giving you a constant source of revenue, but it also isn't requiring any additional work - not too shabby!

In addition to books, artwork, music, intellectual property can include formulas, systems and processes, inventions, licenses, logos and branding designs, and more. Anything that is the fruit of your creativity may be considered intellectual property, but you'll need to decide what you're going to do with your intellectual property in order to derive wealth from it. Figuring out a formula or a system that leverages your intellectual property can really bring in the money for the long term.

The *Chicken Soup for the Soul* series of inspirational books is a prime example of a solid plan for a great piece of intellectual property. The first book was in development for about three years. It was based not simply on one book but rather a formula that the creators sensed would develop into a series of books and perhaps spin off in other directions as well. They knew that every product has a life cycle, so they pre-paved what would replace the first book, then the second, and so on. Their formula created a plan for the original book as well as all future books. The project was self-funded and the process was arduous, but as I'm sure you know, their efforts were (and continue to be) richly rewarded.

Tip #90: Salary Sacrifice Now for a More Secure Retirement

If you are employed and pay tax, consider salary sacrificing into your super or retirement fund to boost the amount of funds available to you in your retirement years. A regular contribution, even if it's small, can make a tremendous difference in the amount you have to live off of at retirement, especially if you start now. Another benefit: recent changes in some areas to the amount of tax you owe on money paid into your retirement fund may make this an even better way to invest in your future. Contact your account to learn what's going on in your jurisdiction.

You may also be able to use the cash in your retirement fund to buy some good long-term investments, such as shares in real estate or solid companies with strong reputations. When you increase the overall performance of the cash in your retirement fund, the result will be a bigger and better nest egg for you and your loved ones when you do retire.

Since you obviously want to make the most of your retirement fund, it's in your best interests to educate yourself about the investment options available to you. Spend some time planning how much you're able to contribute to your retirement fund each month, and how much of that you'd like to invest. Even if you're choosing very low-risk investments with compound interest, you'll still be growing your money faster than just letting it sit in the bank. Remember that it's important to make that money grow faster than the rate of inflation so that the passage of time doesn't eat away at your hard-earned savings.

To find out more about investment opportunities and saving wisely for your retirement, make sure you consult with a licensed financial advisor who is authorized to give advice on superannuation. A good advisor will help you put aside the right amount of money in the right places to optimize growth and help ensure a secure future for you in your later years.

Tip #91: Join Associate and Affiliate Programs

Associate programs and affiliate programs are a wonderful way for you to earn passive income simply by sharing products and services that you think are fantastic. The concept is simple: when someone you've told about a company makes a purchase at that company, that company rewards you for helping them bring in a new customer. Many companies set up these types of programs because they know that word-of-mouth advertising is the best way to develop a solid reputation and grow their businesses.

Nowadays there are all kinds of associate programs out there for you to get involved in. One example is the Christopher Howard Company Associate Program, which offers a variety of awards ranging from self-development and business courses all the way to cash credits. All you have to do is tell people about the business and then earn commissions when sales are made to those people. You can find hundreds more associate programs in virtually every industry imaginable simply by going to your favorite search engine and typing in "associate programs" or "affiliate programs."

In the unlikely event that you don't find an associate program that suits you, be proactive and build your own website to sell other people's products. Charge a commission and you'll be earning cash for every item sold via your website. You can start your own website these days with very little money upfront and basically no technological ability. All it takes is a computer with Internet access and a little determination!

If you have your own products to sell, setting up an affiliate or associate program is a great way to increase your sales and market presence without having to actually hire additional sales representatives. Your affiliates will go out and market your products on your behalf in exchange for a percentage of the sales they generate; it's a win-win scenario. If money is tight for you, this just could be the solution you need to generate more income without having to shell out any more cash.

I myself know and implement the power of associate and affiliate marketing. I am always looking for people to market my products for me, either online or by word-of-mouth, because I understand just how powerful a marketing tool enthusiastic associates truly are. I also take advantage of being an associate myself by stocking other people's products on my own website.

Tip #92: Be Flexible in Order to Get a Better Job

It may seem impossible to get into your desired industry, company, or job, especially if you have little or no experience. However, there are a few clever tricks you can try that just may steer you to the right path.

First of all, realize that patience is a virtue. If you don't have the skills or the contacts necessary to land your dream job, then you'll need to find a job a little lower down on the corporate ladder. Apply to all the jobs you can that are as close as possible to the job you actually want so that you can learn the tools you need to learn, impress the people you need to impress, and establish a level of credibility and work ethic that will eventually earn you the spot you really want. Yes, it will take some time, but during that time you'll learn a lot while receiving a steady paycheck. Remember, even if it's only a temporary or contract position, it can still help you on your career path. I myself have found many permanent roles by starting out in temporary positions first.

If you don't have enough experience or education to get anywhere near your desired field, don't fret! There are plenty of jobs out there that require no experience and - believe it or not -can still help you get your foot in the door of your dream job. Many of my friends and I have found work as telemarketers, restaurant servers, postal advertisement deliverers... the list goes on. The pay can be pretty ordinary and the conditions challenging, but these jobs are usually easier to get and most will actually teach you some of the skills you'll need for the job you truly want.

For example, if you get a job waiting tables, you're learning more than just how to bring food to somebody. You're also learning how to multitask (keeping a ten-table section happy isn't easy!), to hone your customer service skills, to handle money correctly, and to be highly organized and efficient. Those skills you learned in the restaurant will most certainly prove beneficial in another job later on. You might use those your talent for customer service as a human resources director or your superior organizational skills as an office manager or entrepreneur.

When you learn something in one situation that can be of use to you in another, this is called a "transferable skill." Transferable skills are extremely important to you because they will help you show potential employers that you have what it takes to do a job even though you may not have the precise experience they're looking for. When you're ready to apply for that job you've always wanted, really emphasize your transferable skills to show your future boss you've got the right skill set for the job.

If you are having trouble getting a paying job, often employers will take on an enthusiastic volunteer who is willing to either put in some time for free or work for a share of any extra income they bring into the business. Working under these terms will allow you to show yourself off, meet people who might be able to help your career further, and build up a resume of experience. Not only is it a great way to get involved in a field, but it also gives you an opportunity to show the right people how serious you are and how hard you'll work to get what you want. These are qualities that immediately impress any potential employer and are sure to lead to more lucrative opportunities down the road

Chapter 8: Growing Your Own Business

Let me start by saying that I know you are a talented person. I know this because everyone in this world has a unique talent, something that he or she was born to share with the world.

Perhaps you're already getting paid for your talents. Perhaps you have a talent but haven't found a way to monetize it yet. Regardless of what your talent actually is, i want you start thinking about a way to turn it into a steady stream of reliable, sustainable income.

If generating your income on your own sounds appealing to you, trust me when I say that I know just how you feel. What more rewarding way could there be to earn fabulous wealth doing something that you love?

Tip #93: Building and Sustaining Your Business

Let's say you are a trained massage therapist. You get paid a certain amount for 30 or 60 minutes of your time. The massage therapists I know make a pretty good living, so maybe you're doing okay or even better than okay. But what happens if you go away on a holiday or if your child stays home sick from school or you trip and sprain your wrist?

For most self-employed people, when they get taken out of the game, their business gets taken out of the game, too. If for whatever reason you're unable to take care of your clients at any given time, your business' bottom line takes a direct hit.

Being on call for your business 100 percent of the time can be stressful. It can also take its toll on your bank account when you're unable to work. That's why I encourage you to build your current business into something more than it already is. I'm not talking about going crazy here and buying expensive advertising time during prime time television or renting a boutique space in your local shopping mall (although maybe that would work wonders for you!). What I am talking about is finding ways to keep your business going even when you need a break. Perhaps that will entail hiring an employee or an assistant. Perhaps it will mean taking on a partner to share your business with.

Let's go back to the massage therapist example: if, as a massage therapist, you do end up with a wrist sprain, wouldn't it be amazing to have an employee - say, a new massage therapist graduate who needs to increase his practice hours - who could take over your clients until you had recovered? Of course, your employee would have to be compensated for his time, but you could take a cut because you found him the business and perhaps also because he isn't experienced enough to earn what you earn. As your business grows, you could give the work you can't handle yourself over to him and take a commission for generating business on his behalf.

This type of employee scenario is great because you wouldn't have to pay an hourly wage; you would only pay the person when he or she actually performed work for you. You could even set up a similar scenario with a partner in which each of you agree to take care of the other's business when that person is busy or otherwise unavailable. Sure, you wouldn't earn extra income that way, but there are plenty of other benefits, the most important of which being that your business doesn't stop when you have to.

If your business is viable without you, even for a little while, it's better than your business being totally dependent upon your availability and performance. If you have to put clients on hold when you're ill or on holidays, they won't appreciate it and your business' reputation will surely suffer. By having a contingency plan in place for when you're unavailable, your business can keep humming along and your client base and reputation can grow right along with it.

One other way to make money from your growing business is to sell it. If you want out of your business, consider advertising it for sale. People will happily pay a lot of money for a ready-made business with an established reputation and client base. You've done all the hard work of getting it started; now all a buyer has to do is come in and keep it going. Selling your business may be just the ticket to getting the fast cash you need.

Tip #94: Where's Your Website?

If you are freelancing or doing any contract work of any kind, you absolutely need to have a bit of cyber real estate of your own. A small simple website is fine; you don't need something fancy to advertise your services.

Your website should offer a place for potential clients to find you online and learn a little bit about the work that you do - enough to entice them to make contact. Choose a format that fits your personality and appeals to your target market. Consider the people that will be visiting the site: what kind of look will they expect to see? What information are they going to need?

Every successful website needs the following pages:

- ☐ *About Us* - This page will give a very brief description of your business and your personal background. Include a photo because it will personalize the experience for people and make it more likely they'll reach out to you.
- ☐ *Products/Services* - Let people know what you do. Include photos if possible. Remember this is a sales pitch, so do your best to market your wares as favorably as possible!
- ☐ *Pricing* - Not everyone will want to post these details online; what you choose to do will depend on what type of business you're in. If you don't state prices, be aware that some people find this frustrating and it will cause them to seek elsewhere.

Check in with other people in your industry; if everyone is listing their prices and you aren't, you may be putting your website (and your business) at a disadvantage. Also, consider offering bundles, special deals, or sales offers. Everyone loves a bargain!

- *Portfolio* - Include the highlights of your career, with photos where possible. The idea is to "wow" people so don't bore them with mundane choices. Showcase your portfolio items that really shine! (By the way, if you don't have a portfolio, get one. You can increase your number of portfolio samples simply by doing some work for free, either for others or just to put in your portfolio... but always make sure potential clients have something to look at.)
- *Testimonials* - These are always a good idea. I like having a testimonials page but also showcasing a few of the best right there on your home page. This draws people in by showing that you're experienced and that you do a tremendous job.
- *Contact Us* - Offer your email address, phone number, and/or an online contact form so people can get a hold of you however they prefer.
- *FAQs* - Your Frequently Asked Questions page serves two purposes: first, it preemptively answers a lot of the questions that may be on your prospective clients' minds; second, it is a natural place to include lots of keywords related to your business,

which will make it easier to find you on search engines like Google. For example, if you are a ghostwriter, in your FAQs you might have questions such as "What is a ghostwriter?" and "How much do ghostwriters cost?" because these are terms people might use when searching for your type of business.

- *Blog* - Again, the purpose of a blog is twofold. Most important is that updating your site regularly (I recommend weekly or more) is the best way to get found on Google. Also, blogging is a great way to keep people engaged with your website because the content is always fresh. You can blog about your latest projects, trends in your industry, money-saving tips... whatever you believe your website visitors will be interested in.
- *Home Page* - I saved this page for last because the best home page is one that has elements of all the pages above and is extremely easy to navigate. Your home page should have obvious links to your other pages as well as one or two testimonials in a prominent place and a quick bit about what you do. Don't forget to use your company logo as a header for your website. I recommend putting your blog on your home page as an easy way to get your news right in front of your readers and ensure that your busiest site page is always evolving.

As you can see, you don't need a whole lot to set up your website. In fact, getting your site up and running is so easy that many companies allow you to do it yourself for free.

Check out Wordpress (at www.Wordpress.org). They have amazing free templates and their backend is super user-friendly, which means you can probably set your site up all by yourself even if you aren't tech-savvy.

Aside from all these details, remember to always keep your reader in mind as you build the site. Tell them what you can do to improve their lives or solve their problems. That's how you win clients - by making it clear what excellent value they'll be getting for their money. Also ensure that the site is a good reflection of who you are and what you do. Being honest and having an attitude of service will always work in your favor.

Tip #95: Revitalize Your Business Profits

As a fellow businessperson, I know that you are always looking for ways to grow your business, boost sales, and increase profits. There is lots of good advice out there that can and does fill many shelves full of many books!

Are there any ideas you've stumbled upon over the years that you could now take action on in order to make some fast cash? People come up with good ideas all the time, but unfortunately many of those good ideas fall by the wayside as the everyday routine of doing business sets in. Perhaps you've jotted your ideas down in a notebook somewhere or have been saving inspirational emails.

Now is the time to dig out a few of those ideas and make something exciting happen! I challenge you to think outside the box when it comes to your business, at least for a little while, so that you can open yourself and your business up to the possibility of wonderful and lucrative changes.

Here are just a few questions to get your started:

- Are there any new problems that your clients or community face?
- What new things have your clients been asking for?
- What new, original ways could you be promoting your existing products?
- What new products are there that you could promote (or cross-promote)?
- Is there any new information that you could compile or explain for the community?
- Is there any follow-up that you have been putting off?
- Could you ramp up sales with a special promotion such as a seasonal sale?
- What trends are happening in your industry right now that you could capitalize on?
- Who inspires you? Could you meet with them to brainstorm?
- Could you attend some training or an exciting industry event to update your skills and/or business knowledge?
- Are there any online seminars to participate in or any social networking opportunities to build on?

If you work from home, there can be periods where your imagination and profitability may stagnate. When is the last time that you went out to see what is new in your neighborhood? How about the last time you went to the business district or area pertinent to your niche and explored what was happening there? You'd be surprised at the new ideas and inspiration that come from getting out and looking around.

Another idea: have some fun! We all need to make room for fun every day. It is a great way to keep things light and to keep yourself grounded. Fun will relax you, refresh you, and help you to see things from a different angle. When was the last time you pumped up your favorite music and danced around the house or bounced on a trampoline or literally stopped to smell the roses? Try it... and expect to be delighted by the results.

Tip #96: Widening Your Profit Margins

Getting richer in business is all about increasing income and/or reducing expenses. Yes, I'm sure you know this already, but it bears repeating because sometimes all you need to make more money in business is a fresh look at the way you're doing things.

What could you be doing differently to lower your fixed costs? Smaller fixed expenses reduce your break-even point and improve profitability. The latest and greatest way to reduce your fixed costs is by growing your online presence. Because the Internet has a global reach, it is easier to advertise for less while actually reaching more people. A website is your ultimate marketing tool; it often works better than any other form of advertising but costs relatively little or is sometimes even free.

Another option for reducing your expenses may be to outsource. Outsourcing converts fixed costs to variable costs, so your break-even point may improve significantly. Consider outsourcing everything, including yourself by becoming a vendor that provides services on a contract basis.

What about more obvious fixed costs, such as your rent and utility payments? Could you move to less expensive offices? Are you running the air conditioners too much? Is there a better deal on pens, paper, and other supplies somewhere? Could you be scanning and emailing instead of spending money on photocopiers? A practical look at the everyday costs of doing business may be just what you need to improve your profitability.

You may even be able to convert some of your employees' wages from a fixed cost to a variable cost, at least to an extent. Perhaps there is an opportunity to compensate them with stock options or give them smaller salaries but larger bonuses based on performance. You'll have to crunch the numbers for your individual situation but it may be a fantastic way to improve your bottom line.

Of course, the flip side to increasing your profits is growing your income - and the most obvious way to do that is to raise your prices. It may sound scary, but guess what? Some items sell even better when you up the price thanks to a little phenomenon called "prestige pricing."

In essence, prestige pricing means that when you price your products too low, people tend to believe they aren't worth much and are therefore less interested in making purchases. Conversely, if you up your price to a level that makes people say to themselves, "Wow, this thing must be great if it costs this much!" then more browsers turn into buyers because they believe in the value of what you're selling.

Another way to widen your margins is to improve the quality of your product. While it may seem more expensive at the outset, in many cases selling a higher quality product means less effort marketing, fewer customer complaints and therefore more customers, less money spent on product repairs or recalls, etc.

Another strong tactic is to create fixed sales. In other words, if you can find regular customers who make ongoing orders, you'll have a steadier stream of income and operations will become more predictable and therefore more efficient. As a result, you may be able to spend that extra time branching out into newer ventures or drumming up new clients for your existing business.

Tip #97: Bring in New Business by Offering Equity or Profit Sharing

Offering a share in the profits is a great way to motivate people to get involved in your business. Whether you're starting a new company or you've already got one off and running, you'll likely come to a point where you'd like to grow your business, but you're lacking the cash flow. Profit sharing or equity offerings through stocks or other means can entice every stakeholder in your business - suppliers, employees, customers - to contribute financially in exchange for a piece of the pie.

These deals can be structured in the traditional fashion of cash upfront in exchange for a percentage of ownership or of the profits. However, you can also get a little more creative with your deals. Try offering customers cash incentives for bringing in new business. Ask for discounts from your suppliers in exchange for stock, a prolonged contract, or positive referrals to your associates in the industry. Offer your employees shares in your business instead of raises so they are motivated to work harder to increase not just your profits, but theirs too.

Not all of these suggestions will bring you cash directly, but they will either reduce your costs or increase your revenue (or both), which eventually translates into more money in the bank for you. Always keep your stakeholders in the loop so they can be as excited about your business as you are. The more comfortable they are with you and your company's operations, the more eager they will be to invest in your business when it's time to expand or take on a big new project. Remember also that any business arrangement, including equity or profit sharing deals, should be carefully planned, legally documented, and delivered on time to ensure not only your plan's ongoing success, but also your good reputation.

What's great about profit sharing and equity deals is that they can be cheap to organize and allow you to fund your business projects without any cash upfront from you. You simply need to talk to people about the benefits of investing in your business; they will be the ones to provide the capital you need to get your business growing. Another nice thing is that these types of deals are almost never permanent. If your business is really flourishing and you want to buy your investors out, you can do so relatively easily (as long as you've set up your agreement as such). Then you'll once again have all of your business' profits to yourself.

Tip #98: Make Some Noise With Viral Marketing

Viral marketing employs the power of word of mouth and its younger, hipper cousin, social media. It can move an idea, product, business, or individual from obscurity into the global spotlight in days, sometimes in mere hours. Viral marketing is all about Facebook, Twitter, and YouTube. It's about creating awareness about a person, place, or thing and generating a lot of excitement around it.

So what exactly is the type of content that tends to go viral and spread like wildfire across the World Wide Web?

The following are ideas that have all been used time and again to create a viral message. Could you incorporate one of these into your business?

- A funny or shocking video
- A free product or service
- Free information
- A free workshop, seminar or online course
- Anything extraordinary (I mean really, really extraordinary)

Make sure that your content is interesting, content-rich and provides value - even if that value is just giving someone a good laugh. Remember that social media isn't as much about earning money directly as it is about nurturing the personal connections between your business and its clients and colleagues, which will likely grow your profits in time. Your content doesn't even have to relate directly to your business as long as it's a fun or unique idea that will generate some buzz.

In your content, always include links back to your website and to your opt-in page. Tell those visitors who download or watch your content to spread the word. Do your part by sharing your best links on your Facebook and Twitter pages, as well as in your email (you can put the link in your signature line or actually send out a special email notifying people of your new, cool content).

You may also want to consider employing a pay-per-click campaign. Advertising your content on Google is a great way to get some exposure. Of course, if your content truly does go viral, advertising will no longer be necessary. In the meantime, however, a bit of light advertising never hurts!

Tip #99: Expert Insight From Dr. Joanna Martin

The 7 Keys to a Profitable and Effective Sales Presentation, by Marketing Guru Joanna Martin

Effective selling is a powerful skill that everyone can learn with a little practice. Here's a sneak peek at my tried-and-true seven-step program for sales presentation success:

- *Create Connection: Become a welcome guest and inspire trust and responsiveness in your audience.*

If you are serious about inspiring people to buy your product, you have to realize that you are not actually selling your product at all - you are selling yourself.

The first two minutes you spend on stage are crucial; you will use them to establish trust and rapport. You have to remember that the first thing you say, your "opening," is like your headline. It must capture your whole crowd. If you lose them at this time you will RARELY re-capture their attention. Go for 100 percent involvement.

To create connection, try one or some combination of these approaches:

- *Ask enrolling questions: Open by asking questions that 100 percent of the audience will answer "yes" to, such as "Who here would like to increase their sales, by a show of hands?"*

- *Engage them in an activity, such as turning to the person next to them and saying, "You're in the right place," or get them up to meet three people they haven't met yet. By doing this you take the pressure off yourself to have to rev them up. What's more, they usually have a bit of a laugh during the process, which puts them in a nice receptive state for your message.*

- *Tell a GOOD joke: I have seen people use humor very effectively to capture their crowd. This takes a bit of finesse and a certain personality style, so it requires a healthy dose of confidence. It's not for everyone!*

- *Blow them away with facts and stats: I have seen people start presentations using undeniable facts and stats, followed by a benefit-focused outline of their talk.*

- *Get Permission to Do Your Thing: Demonstrate credibility and earn the right to be speaking to your audience by illustrating your past results as powerfully as possible.*

You must get permission from your audience to speak to them and ultimately to sell to them, too.

There are four key elements to this step:

- ☐ *Explain your style. If it's your first time - tell them. They'll love you for your courage. If you want audience interaction, tell them - they'll know what to expect. I personally always make a point of telling my audience we'll be having a bit of fun while we learn as I tend to be a bit crazy on stage from time to time!*

- ☐ *Confirm your position as the expert. The key here is your credibility statement. Why on earth should these people bother to listen to you? Once you have an answer to this question, you just need to reveal this information to them in a powerful way. Things to think about as you create a credibility statement:*
- ☐ *What's your story or hook?*
- ☐ *What specific results have you achieved that prove your credibility?*
- ☐ *Have you got any testimonials that prove your credibility?*
- ☐ *Get buy-in for what you're going to teach them. It makes sense to give your audience an overview of how you are actually going to teach. Your aim with this step is to have them desperate to know what you know. You want them to agree that they NEED to know what you are about to share.*
- ☐ *Get permission for the sale upfront. Think about it. If a friend asks you, "Can I talk to you about something?" what do you usually do? Most of us say, "Sure!" and then sit down to listen. It's the same for your presentation. If you ask*

permission, your audience will respond like a friend and take notice, plus they will respect how polite you are, which will endear you to them.

- *Engage With Your Content: Decide on the action you want the audience to take, and craft the backbone of your presentation with this end in mind.*

This is the part of the presentation when you should teach something. Deliver value. There is no such thing as too much content, only a too complicated delivery. When designing the backbone of your presentation there are some key things to ask yourself:

- Who is your audience?
- What level of experience do they have?
- What are their needs, wants, fears, and frustrations?
- What are they desperate to know?
- What's their biggest problem?
- What's their greatest dream?

Make sure you tailor your presentation to your audience members to maximize the perceived value of your presentation.

- *Establish Need: Create dissatisfaction in your audience by illustrating where they are versus where they want to be. There are two ways to make this work:*

- *Pain Motivated: You identify your audience's pain, aggravate it, rub some salt in the wound, and then demonstrate how your product will take their pain away. This is moving them from "pain" to "no problems."*
- *Inspiration Motivated: You paint a bright, inspiring vision of the future and point out all of the wonderful things that would be possible for them in this new future. You then demonstrate how far from this "ideal" they are currently. This is moving them from "no problems" to "inspiration."*

- *Reveal the Product and Build Tension: Give a benefit-driven description of your product to build up the value. Before your presentation, think long and hard about your product and how you will package it to create an offer that is irresistibly compelling for your audience that it becomes a "no-brainer."*

Things to think about when designing your offer:

1. *Who is your audience and what do they want from you?*
2. *What price point is reasonable based on what you know of your audience?*

3. *What is the central product: CDs, DVDs, books, seminars, consulting, other services...?*

4. *What bonuses could you add to build the value to an extreme level? Always be thinking about bonuses that have high perceived value to the customer, but low cost for you to deliver. Endeavor to come up with enough good quality bonuses that the value of the bonuses exceeds the value of the actual product.*

5. *Could you make a two-tiered offering, perhaps a basic version of your pack and a deluxe version with an extra special bonus or two? This transitions your audience from thinking, "Do I buy or not?" to "Which package do I buy?"*

While revealing your product, continue to build tension. By this stage, your audience should be feeling a little uncomfortable, and that's good. They are aware of the fact that they are not getting the results they deserve.

This segment is the substance of the close. During this segment you can introduce:

- *What problem does your product solve?*
- *The name of your product.*
- *Who it's for.*
- *Who it's* not *for.*

- *A benefit-focused description of what it does and what it includes.*
- *Proof that what you say is true (testimonials are ideal for this).*

6. *Make a No-Brainer Offer: Package up your product with bonuses, create urgency, and remove risk.*

You MUST deliver this part of the presentation with just as much passion as you did the backbone. Although you are revealing information about the product, your focus should still be on BUILDING TENSION.

Include a good reason why they should buy now. You can't just say, "There are only 10 spots, so hurry now." Instead, say something like: "Because we only have room for nine more clients on our books, I am going to make an offer, which will be available for the first nine of you who choose to take action immediately." Employ the law of scarcity; people want what they can't have. When designing your offer, think about what "limiter" you can put on it to enhance the sense of scarcity.

- *Invite Immediate Action: Finish powerfully with a commanding invitation to buy.*

Once you've outlined and inspired people with your offer, you have to tell them exactly *what to do. The reason for this is that if you've done a good job with the connection step, they might not want to be rude and break the connection to go and buy what you're offering. Therefore you must invite them to buy.*

I like to use "embedded commands" at this stage. An embedded command is a three-step command where the first two steps tell you how to do it and the last step tells you what to do.

Here's an example:

"I invite you right now to close your notebook, run to the back, and register for this seminar."

Warning: *I have seen countless presentations come unstuck at this point. Once you have delivered your invitation to action, SHUT UP AND GET OFF STAGE! Do not take questions. Do not ask anyone else to speak. Just thank them for their time, tell them where you'll be and close the session. DON'T WIMP OUT! Your delivery must be punchy and roll off the tongue with confidence and certainty.*

This profit principle is an extract from my full Blueprint In Action Series *and is just one of 7 profit principles which make up my 7-step tried and tested proven formula to adding multiple streams of income through speaking for your business. Learn more at:*

www.shiftspeakertraining.com/p/getthefullblueprint

Tip #100: Find a Problem and Be the Solution

I recently moved house and found that I had a big job at the other end with all the boxes to unpack, cupboards to fill, and closets to organize. I quickly realized that there were surprisingly few professional unpackers in the phone listings. The ones I could find were booked solid for weeks ahead. Aside from the fact that many were work-from-home moms who didn't run their businesses every day, they told me that there were so many people who needed help organizing their homes and offices, they had regular monthly jobs and very little time for new clients! I was amazed that no one else was offering a service like this when the demand was so high, especially considering it would take virtually no money or effort to get started.

There are thousands of examples just like this one; all it takes is a little creativity and a keen eye to spot them. People have little problems every day that they would gladly pay someone to help them solve. Start looking at other people's problems as potential money-makers for you, and you'll be well on your way to a brand new stream of income.

You could offer a one-off spring cleaning service for homes that may turn into a regular cleaning job, or contact small businesses that could use help sorting out their files, receipts, or other paperwork. Try putting up flyers around the neighborhood for snow removal, leaf raking, or lawn mowing. The amount of seasonal work like this is astronomical; the demand is so high that you shouldn't have trouble finding work.

Here's another great example: I recently saw a truck on the road with the words "Graffiti Removal" painted in large letters along with the contact phone number. Now, I happen to know from experience that there are solutions you can buy from industrial cleaning suppliers that dissolve graffiti so that it can be washed off with water. It's a bit of information that most people don't know and is a great money making opportunity for anyone with an entrepreneurial spirit. Graffiti is a frustrating problem for schools, downtown businesses, industrial parks, and even many residential areas. This truck also had listed on it the other businesses its owners provided, so everywhere it was parked or driven, it advertised its unique services to hundreds of people.

All of these are clever-but-easy businesses that have been set up to solve the problems of others. If you don't know where to start, just take some time to do a bit of brainstorming. Don't be afraid to copy the ideas of others - it only takes a couple of phone calls to find out if there's enough demand in the market for another competitor. Once you've settled on an idea, create some professional-looking leaflets to post in the neighborhood or drop in people's mailboxes. Include a couple of rave reviews from friends or past customers, and don't forget to clearly communicate your contact information. Get a message service if you aren't available to pick up the phone at all times. Finally, do your best to do a good job and charge competitively. This will turn your customers into repeat clients who enthusiastically recommend you to others.

Tip #101: Creating Your Own Marketable Product

Creating your own product may sound daunting, but the reality is that inside of you is a huge store of creative energy just waiting to be manifested into something useful and meaningful. It's not as difficult as it sounds to create a new product. Most new inventions these days are just slightly smarter variations of existing products.

When I was a teenager, I had a huge collection of dangly earrings. To prevent me from losing them or getting them all tangled together, my mom gave me an old window screen she wasn't using anymore. I hung my dozens of pairs of earrings in the screen's webbing, delighted that I could both see my entire collection and know that they were paired neatly together, safe and sound. Years later, products started showing up in accessory stores that were exactly what my mom had given me - an old window screen - but instead they were painted in pretty colors and stapled on to ornate, feminine frames. I remember thinking, "Why didn't I think of that? I could have made a fortune!"

What good ideas are you using in your home to make life easier? Could these ideas work for others, too? Commit yourself to carefully analyzing your activities over the next week or so to see what ingenious ideas you've incorporated into your daily routine without even noticing. Once you've come up with one or two good ones, start planning how you can get those ideas to market.

Consider creating an e-book, which can be a great money-maker. Similarly, you can create downloadable .mp3 or video files to teach people how to solve certain types of problems. Your product will usually reflect your individual areas of expertise, so ask yourself what you do well enough to share with others. Are you a great cook? Do you have an eye for interior decorating? What skills do you have that you could transform into a marketable product to sell for years to come?

If you're having trouble identifying some of your special skills, try this technique instead: think about the major problems your society is facing today. In every developed country in the world, we're facing personal problems like depression, insomnia, and stress. Working parents struggle to find spaces in quality day homes for their children. Adults of all ages are turning to their spiritual sides and trying to learn how to nurture that aspect of themselves. What products could you create to address these issues?

One good idea is to host a support group, either online or at home. Members who subscribed would get unlimited attendance to meetings, an area to discuss freely with individuals facing the same problems, and a regular newsletter (weekly or monthly, for example) providing insight, support, and guidance.

If the task of creating something that solves the problems of others and then getting it to market still seems too overwhelming, try involving a trusted friend or colleague to start the venture with you. Chances are you'll have skills that complement each other so that you don't have to take on the whole big burden all by yourself. Get together with your partner and write up a business plan to work out all the kinks before you invest too much time or money.

If you've hit on a really super idea that is simply beyond your reach to realize, write the business plan anyway, and then sell it to someone else. There are plenty of venture capitalists out there with an eye for spotting those great investments. Just make sure that, whether you're involved in the development of your idea or not, you settle on a price and/or profit sharing plan that you're happy with.

Tip #102: Create New Products With Added Value

Go to your local markets and scout around for creative ideas that are selling well. Which products are popular with which types of buyers? Which ideas could you implement in your own business? Often all it takes is a little inspiration from sellers who are doing well to revitalize your own sales and profit margins.

I have done this type of thing with many products. For example, I once started buying two-dollar pairs of children's plastic shoes and gluing pieces of feather boas or marabou onto them. It was an easy, inexpensive way to create play shoes with a boudoir charm for little girls. My little idea was very popular; I sold the shoes for ten dollars a pair, turning my small investment into some pretty serious profits. Encouraged by the strong sales of the shoes, I decided to make bags with matching trim. When those did well I also made hats and gloves, and then made them into gift packs with bath bombs and hairbrushes. It was a little play beauty parlor in one delightful package, and I made a lot of money by making and selling those wonderfully simple sets.

My sets sold well because each time I added a product, I created new value for my customers. These inexpensive add-ons greatly increased both my profit margin and my customer satisfaction (because my buyers always felt like they were getting more and more for their money).

What added value could you include with the products or services you sell? Where could you sell them for maximum exposure to buyers? It's easy to increase your success potential with value add-ons and good visibility to your potential customers. Take your value-added products to sell at places where your customers will most likely be looking for you. For instance, I sold my children's products at school fundraisers, family markets, and through newspapers and magazines targeted to families and parents. All it took was some creative add-ons and a bit of marketing.

In fact, you don't even need to have an established business to make money with value add-ons. Take my example: I didn't have expensive start-up costs and I didn't need my own dedicated retail store. All I really had was an idea about how to make a fun children's product inexpensively. You must have some of these types of ideas floating around, too, so take some time to brainstorm.

Other ways to add value include gifts-with-purchase; offering related classes, seminars, or lessons for customers who use your products or services; offering discounts for multiple purchases... the list goes on and on. Many of these ideas won't cost you a thing but can greatly increase your cash flow, which is exactly what you'll need to bail yourself out of a sticky financial situation.

Tip #103: Maximize Work Opportunities

Work: the first and foremost way that we make money! Let's deconstruct this model so that we can see how to maximize our efforts here.

We exchange value in the form of time, skills, labor, and/or activities for money (or some other kind of comparable compensation). Trading our value for another kind of value is our reward for working.

Have you ever stopped to wonder why someone pays you to work? No matter what kind of job your doing, usually you get money from people for one of the following reasons:

- They have money and aren't interested in doing the work themselves.
- They have money and don't have the skill set to do the work themselves.
- They have money and a desire to delegate the work to someone else because of the size of the project or a constraint on their part.

By understanding the basic reasons that people pay you for the value that you offer, you can begin to capitalize on your work opportunities in ways that you may not have previously considered.

For example, you could suggest to your boss to send any of his whiners, complainers, or lazy workers to report to you. It isn't a promotion and you wouldn't be their new boss or supervisor, but your boss may readily agree to your offer anyway because then your boss would no longer be the one to have to handle that stressful annoyance. Your offer will likely enhance your value as an employee in your boss' eyes and a healthy raise might just be on the horizon!

In this example,you are providing value by taking a task from someone who can afford to pay you and would prefer to delegate to someone else. What real life examples could you put into practice in your life? Are there some very unpleasant jobs at work that people don't want to take on? What about the "can't do" jobs? Is there something that is required or could be valuable in your organization that nobody else can do?

Examples of "can't do" jobs you might be able to handle would be if your boss could use an interpreter for a Chinese client and you happen to speak Mandarin. Or perhaps your company's website is shamefully outdated and you are skilled at creating simple websites. Think of the value you could add by stepping in with a unique skill that nobody else at your office can do.

When it comes to maximizing opportunities at work, definitely make sure that part of the maximizing process includes a boost in pay. This may come in the form of a raise, but you might also be paid in stock options, extra vacation time, or simply bonus money earned on a contractual basis each time you fulfill one of these unique needs. Make sure you understand the new value you are contributing to the company you work for and work out something with your employer ahead of time so that you are compensated fairly.

Tip #104: Direct Sales Consulting

A friend of mine, Cheryl, disgruntled with the corporate world, was introduced to an opportunity to sell a particular makeup line. Never a girly girl, she didn't know much about makeup and the wide variety out there in the brightly lit boutique shops. Nevertheless, she was won over by the product, the marketing collaterals, and the company ethic.

Eager to leave Corporate America behind, she dove into the new opportunity headfirst, signed up, paid her startup fees and got busy talking about the products. She threw parties and carried business cards and samples with her wherever she went. She flew across the country to attend every convention and company event. She enticed friends and acquaintances to sign up to her "downline."

What happened to Cheryl? In fact, she has become wildly successful. She has built her business both wide and deep and has the Mercedes Benz and annual trips to Hawaii to show for it.

I am thrilled for her because she is living a life that she loves, a life of her own design full of abundant rewards. She is so passionate that she has made success look easy, when actually if you step step back and analyze Cheryl's situation, you'll see that being a direct sales consultant isn't as simple as you might think (despite what their marketing brochures will tell you!).

Success in direct sales consulting takes a certain type of person with a specific skill set. Firstly, being highly social will dramatically increase your odds of success. Talking to people is what it's all about: networking, developing new connections, and making the most of every relationship. You have to honestly love having sales parties and to encourage others to do the same. You need to be willing to enlist and train others to succeed in order to aid your own business.

But the ultimate key to success as a direct sales consultant is truly believing in the products that you are promoting, as well as the company that stands behind them. When you believe in what you're selling, you automatically become a better salesperson.

The company that Cheryl set up shop with had, and still has, a very solid business model it shares with its reps. Their catalogues and website are well done, informative, and sleek. The company is reputable and they offer great training information. All of this will be critical to your own success because even a fantastic product won't sell if the business model isn't up to par.

Direct sales consulting opportunities abound, but before you get swept up in one of them, give yourself a serious reality check and do your homework on the company that has caught your eye. Go online to read reviews from existing and former consultants. Then, ask yourself what you actually think about their products and if you really feel you'd be able to sell them.

Check in with yourself by answering the following questions:

- Are you social enough?
- Do you love meeting new people?
- Are you a self-motivated go-getter?
- Can you survive with a fluctuating income that is based solely on commission?
- Can you afford, without stress, all the startup costs?
- Do you have the time to invest in getting started? (Keep in mind that you probably won't make a lot of money at first.)
- Do you feel passionate about the products you'd be selling?
- Do you believe in the company, what it stands for, and how it is run?
- What kind of support does the company offer its sales consultants? WIll that be enough for you?

- Is the compensation package/commission scale reasonable and rewarding? You know your financial goals and how much time and effort you have to invest. Does this opportunity fit into your plans?

Before you sign up to be a direct sales consultant, definitely go to at least one of the sales parties. Do you feel comfortable there? Are you having fun with the people in attendance (the host as well as the guests)? Can you envision yourself taking charge of a similar event? If so, does the prospect excite and inspire you?

Most importantly, come armed to the party with a list of questions for the consultant who will be running the show. Ask if he or she is happy in her business and how high the profits are. Don't be embarrassed about asking these so-called "personal questions." This is a real business you may be getting into, not just a series of parties. Doing your due diligence by asking the tough questions is the responsible thing to do. Also, keep in mind that the consultant you chat with will likely get a commission if you sign up to be a consultant thanks to his or her referral and may even earn a percentage of all of your future profits. This is a business transaction, not a sorority gathering - ask the questions!

If you are still intrigued by the idea of becoming a direct sales consultant, I have a feeling you might really have what it takes to be a success! There are direct sales consulting opportunities in all kinds of fun industries, such as:

- Cosmetics
- Clothing
- Bakeware
- Gift wrap
- Gourmet foods
- Health products
- Candles
- Scrapbooking
- Adult toys (yes, even these!)

Tip #105: Get Advertisers on Your Site

Advertising is an easy and fairly predictable way to make money on your website. There are a variety of ways to make money from using space on your website for banner or text advertisements. How much you make from selling space to advertisers will depend on how much traffic your website gets and what your target demographics are. Even if you're just getting started, however, selling super-cheap advertising space is a good way to get a little steady income and entice businesses on a budget to advertise with you.

To make it a bit easier, especially when your website is new, you can join a banner advertisement network, which allows you to use pre-made ad creatives for your website. These networks sell banner ads to advertisers and then pay you for allowing them to display the ads on your website.

Another way to benefit from advertising revenues is by becoming an affiliate marketer. Join a website like Clickbank, Google Affiliate, Commission Junction, the Amazon Affiliate Program, or ShareASale for free. Then, you apply to promote the businesses that you choose. If the advertiser accepts you as an affiliate, then you will have the right to place a variety of text or banner ads on your site. As an affiliate marketer, you will typically generate income whenever someone clicks through one of your links and then makes a purchase. When that happens, you will be paid a percentage of the sale as a commission.

Some advertisers pay you per click versus per sale, which can be a much easier way to generate regular affiliate income. Typically you'll only be paid a few cents per click, so the key with pay-per-click advertising is a high volume of traffic visiting your site on a consistent basis. Good visibility on the web can take some time, so be patient and stick with it. (Also remember to keep the content on your website fresh by having a blog or something similar. Static sites seldom do well in search rankings.)

Tip #106: Make Money With HubPages

HubPages is a website that allows you to publish your own content and then monetize it. You write about something that you know. Take a tour around and see if it's for you. If so, register for an account and choose a topic. Since it's easier to make money from a specialized or niche topic (because there is typically less competition for people's attention), it's a good idea to make a list of possible niches. Drilling down further and further into your chosen area of interest will lead you to find many possible niches.

Then it's time to do keyword research and assess the level of demand. Just search on the Internet for "free keyword tool" and you'll be able to choose from a variety of website that help you determine which keywords will attract the most search engine traffic. Try to choose a niche that strikes a balance between lots of exposure and minimal competition; it may take some time, but the more research you do, the stronger your new business will be.

Now it's time to put valuable content on your HubPages. Use the keywords that you found during your research to draw traffic to your content. To earn money, place affiliate links and Google Ads in your content (see Tip #105). Every time that a visitor to your HubPage clicks on a link and makes a purchase, you will earn money. It is free to register and get set up on HubPages, so the risk is minimal.

Tip #107: Buy and Sell URLs

Buying and selling website addresses is not difficult at all to do and can actually be quite lucrative. First, you register a domain name (otherwise known as a website address or URL). Then, if somebody really wants that address, you are in a position of power. You can sell it to them or negotiate to take a percentage of the business they do on your URL.

Domain names are often very cheap, but the most straightforward ones are often very expensive because everyone wants their website addresses to be a simple, memorable word or string of words. Some businesses procure many of these, just in case they branch out down the road and have particular names in mind for these various branches. As someone who knows the ins and outs of your business, profession, industry, or hobby, ask yourself whether there any domain names that you could buy today that could shortly be in high demand. If so, you could stand to turn a very tidy and speedy profit.

Can you think of any URLs that are so memorable or catchy that someone would want to own them in order to gain traffic? Again, the best domain names tend to be the simplest. Think of emerging businesses in your area and see if a domain name similar to their own business name is available. All you have to do then is visit a domain name registration site and check to see if one of your great ideas is still up for grabs.

Once you own a website address that you would like to sell, be sure to advertise it by creating a home page (or having one created for you) that has the words "This Domain Name is For Sale" right across the top. Include your contact information so interested parties know whom to get in touch with. For added revenue, include some text or banner advertising (Google AdSense is ideal for this) so you can capitalize on any pay-per-click or pay-per-sale deals that may result from people finding your website. After all, once they get there and realize there isn't a lot going on on your site and/or that it's just up for sale (otherwise known as a "parked domain"), they'll want to move on to a different site. What better way to make money from your little domain by giving them links to click on so they can go where they're interested, compensating you in the process? It's an easy way to generate a bit of passive income you can use to pay down your debts or take care of your monthly expenses.

By the way, you should know that there are people who park domains for a living without trying to sell them. They buy a website URL, set up some simple advertising (usually from Google) and then let people know the site is for sale. Even if no one ever is interested in buying the URL, over time most of these types of sites will generate traffic. The best ones - i.e. the ones with the most intuitive website addresses - can actually get a lot of traffic and therefore a lot of exposure to their pay-per-click or pay-per-sale links. Some people make a good living this way; perhaps you can too!

Tip #108: Setting Up Membership Sites

One of the greatest ways you can convert your website visitors into paying customers is by setting up a membership site. To do this, you'll first need a website with some great free content. The purpose of the free content is to develop a loyal website readership to whom you'll eventually be able to sell website memberships. The more people who see value in your free content, the more people will eventually want to pay for even *better* content.

That's right - in order to have a membership site, you will need to create additional content that is valuable enough that people will want to pay for it. You may either have a bunch of high quality educational articles, videos, or other content, or you might have a message forum where people can post questions and comments and interact with the rest of your community.

The fantastic thing about membership sites is that typically the income is recurring. You charge people a monthly or yearly subscription fee, which is billed to them automatically (no extra work for you), so you can continue to receive ongoing income from each and every subscriber, as opposed to simply a one-time purchase.

You can also capitalize on membership income by offering a newsletter subscription. Again, start by offering free "teaser" content, then build up the value to the point where people will be happy to turn over their money to receive your worthwhile content. When you choose to create a newsletter membership business, you'll need to create a series of emails that people will want to pay for, such as a monthly lesson on a personal growth topic or a weekly email full of the latest coupon codes for popular online retailers.

What knowledge do you already have that you could package as valuable membership content? If you have some great ideas but not the time or ability to get it all written and loaded onto your website or newsletter manager, no problem. This lots of content available online for minimal cost. All you do is purchase it and tweak it for your own purposes (search the Internet for "PLR content" to see what I mean). You could also hire a freelance writer to put together the content for you.

As far as the technological side goes, don't let a lack of computer genius hold you back! Today, you can find extremely user-friendly, intuitive tools online to help you build membership websites and mailing lists without any technical knowledge or expertise. Look online for "Wordpress membership sites" to get started.

The sky is the limit with the concept of membership sites, so sit down and get creative! People will happily pay you good money for quality content. It's simply a matter of matching your unique abilities and insight with an audience who could benefit from what you have to offer.

In Closing...

In reading this book, I sincerely hope you are feeling stronger, more courageous, and inspired to move beyond any money worries you have and into the fabulous realm of personal and financial riches.

Conservative Income or Savings per month

Estimation of Increased Income or Savings Potential From Just A Few of The Ideas In This Book	Per month	Tip No.
Clean out your closets and storage areas (or offer to do someone else's for a fee) and sell excess belongings at local market or on eBay type site a few items per month	$200	Tips 11 - 13
Approach local shops or friends with businesses and offer to sell their surplus stock at local markets or via sites like eBay or Craigslist for a percentage of the sale price.	$200	Tips 14, 15 & 21
Give up a luxury and replace with a luxury that is free but still enjoyable, such as beauty treatments, bought coffee and snacks	$200	Tips 16, 17 & 18

Find trainees to perform the jobs you previously paid full price for or to do jobs others pay you more for.	$200	Tip 19
Hire yourself out as a contractor / tutor / trainer or consultant	$200	Tip 28, 31
Create some e-books on topics of interest to you and sell them on a website (www.HowtoWriteABookThatSells.com) or run a training for your community Bonus tip: Help some other people write e-books and sell them through websites or on your own	$100 $200	Tip 29, 30 & 32
Pick up some handy work in your community, mowing lawns, babysitting, cooking, cleaning, typing, whatever you can do well.	$200	Tip 35
Create a finding money club and create more income or savings	$200	Tip 37
Make your own lunches and make your own coffees and buy in bulk	$200	Tip 41, 42, 49
Shop around and cut back on phone costs, cable TV, movies and utilities – discover your local library and community events	$200	Tip 44 ,45, 58, & 62

Consolidate your credit cards and get a personal loan from the bank, credit union, your employer, friends or family to cut down on crippling credit card interest	$200	Tip 67 - 72
Get a raise, grant, donations or sponsorship to do something extraordinary	$100	Tip 76-79
Total improved cash flow for education/quality of life/mortgage/savings/business growth/etc.	$2,400 month	$28,800 per year
Increase 4 of the above to $500 / month, approx increased income	$1,200	$14,400
Start putting the money into a compounding investment account, understand your taxes, and start growing your 'nest egg'	? ? ?	Tip 22, 23, 52

Please use the ideas in this book as a platform for you to explore your own creativity and personal journey to your wealthy life. It's true that there are over 100 ideas in this book, but there are literally thousands more just waiting for you to discover!

When you *do* discover those beautiful ideas that lead you closer to your financial destiny, please feel free to get in touch and share them with me. I would love to hear your ideas; you can drop me a line at www.MissIndependence.com. You never know - your ideas might just end up in one of my books!

My fondest hope is that this book is of value to you and that you use it as a tool to think creatively and grow your wealth beyond your wildest dreams. I wish you financial independence and unbridled, abundant success!

May you have the very best that this beautiful life has to offer,

~Cydney Turner
www.MillionairesAcademy.com

About the Author

Cydney Turner has been called an "irrepressible entrepreneur." She has been creating and building businesses for over 30 years in a wide variety of industries including food, fashion, IT, stocks and real estate. Her community association, Miss Independence, was founded to help women looking for guidance from ethical experts to create profitable businesses, after her own experience that really good advice was not easy to find, especially for busy mothers already overloaded with responsibilities.

Cydney found that the very best advice usually came from her most successful friends and mentors so her latest project, MillionairesAcademy.com, features trainings and insights from her interviews with successful marketers and mega-millionaires.

She has partnered on many previous projects with other successful entrepreneurs and is featured in the following books:

- *Secrets of Inspiring Women Exposed!* by Dale Beaumont and Emma Lyons

- *Secrets of Stock Market Traders Exposed!* by Dale Beaumont and Warren Stokes
- *Wake Up Women: BE Happy, Healthy and Wealthy!* by Ardice Farrow, Karen Mayfield, and Heidi Reagan
- *The Wonderful Web Women Gold Book 2011* by Janet Beckers
- *Women On Top ...Against the Odds* by Sally Healey and Terri M. Cooper with Dr. Lois Frankel
- *Mumpreneurs Online* by Fiona Lewis
- *Women IGNITING Change* by Tania Usher

In her second book in this series:

Social Wealth Secrets, Accelerated Wealth Strategies for Your Business and Social Media Marketing

Cydney shares the best advice and success strategies for building wealth with social marketing.This book is a guidebook for communication, branding, planning and how to use the extensive online and social mediums available for business today.

She has also partnered on many other projects with successful entrepreneurs and is featured in the following books:

Using her extensive knowledge and experience, her mission in life is to help others unleash their inner millionaire and build a financially secure future for themselves.

As an enthusiastic business founder, real estate investor, and stock market investor, Cydney has made millions and also made costly mistakes, often from taking direction from expensive "experts." This gives her a sympathetic insider position, as a caring mentor, to assist others in taking the required steps toward their own success while avoiding the pitfalls and the sometimes devastating costs of inexperience.

Millionaires Academy is a safe haven where enthusiastic entrepreneurs can find guidance from high integrity, established mentors who are achieving extraordinary results in their areas of expertise. She has aligned with some of the greatest business mentors in the world in order to provide the best advice in a crowded marketplace.

If you are passionate about helping others transform their lives or if you see the benefits of joining a community of like-minded people, and you want to be part of creating solutions that previously would have been out of reach to many of the people who need it the most, then please join the Millionaires Academy Community.

Cydney's mantra is "Dream it! Live it! Love it!"®, based on a lifetime of experience that the secret to success comes down to this very simple formula:

Dare to dream bigger than is comfortable for you, overcome your fear and doubt and begin living into your dream life as though it is already true. Then, as you achieve your success, it is important to review from time to time how far you have come; remember how impossible it seemed once and celebrate and savor your success.

HOW TO WRITE A BOOK THAT SELLS!

Do YOU have a book to write?We invite you to become a published author too.You'll be amazed at the advances in technology that have made publishing a book more affordable than ever before!

We'd like to help you get your message out to the world.

Please join us for your FREE training that will help you plan and write your own book with the best chance of success.

www.HowToWriteABookThatSells.com

-Innovation Publishing –

New York * Las Vegas * Sydney

Made in the USA
Monee, IL
04 November 2026

67386594R00148